D0875300

Asian Interior Design

Asian Interior Design

teNeues

Editor in chief:	Paco Asensio
Editorial coordination:	Haike Falkenberg
Project coordination and text:	Nasple & Asakura
Art director:	Mireia Casanovas Soley
Copyediting:	Matthew Clarkei
Layout:	Gisela Legares Gili
German translation:	Ulrike Fiedler
French translation:	Michel Ficerai

Published by teNeues Publishing Group

teNeues Publishing Company
16 West 22nd Street, New York, NY 10010, USA
Tel.: 001-212-627-9090, Fax: 001-212-627-9511

teNeues Book Division
Kaistraße 18, 40221 Düsseldorf, Germany
Tel.: 0049-(0)211-994597-0, Fax: 0049-(0)211-994597-40

teNeues Publishing UK Ltd.
P.O. Box 402, West Byfleet, KT14 7ZF, Great Britain
Tel.: 0044-1932-403509, Fax: 0044-1932-403514

teNeues France S.A.R.L.
4, rue de Valence, 75005 Paris, France
Tel.: 0033-1-55 76 62 05, Fax: 0033-1-55 76 64 19

teNeues Iberica S.L.
Pso. Juan de la Encina 2-48, Urb. Club de Campo
28700 S.S.R.R., Madrid, Spain
Tel./Fax: 0034-916 595 876

www.teneues.com

ISBN-10:	3-8238-4527-6
ISBN-13:	978-3-8238-4527-0

© 2005 teNeues Verlag GmbH + Co. KG, Kempen

Editorial project: © 2003 LOFT Publications
Via Laietana 32, 4º Of. 92
08003 Barcelona, Spain
Tel.: 0034 932 688 088
Fax: 0034 932 687 073
e-mail: loft@loftpublications.com
www.loftpublications.com

Printed in Spain
October 2005

Special thanks:
Satoshi Asakawa, Tomoko Ihara, Soho China,
Iroje, Mahindra Chawla, APS, Katsuhisa Kida,
Nacása & Partners

Additional photos © Satoshi Asakawa
p.8 Asian Collage, p.11 Bali, p.15 New Delhi,
p.17 Hong Kong, p.21 Beijing,
p.23 Kuala Lumpur, p.27, 29 Shanghai
© Almond Chu p.33

Picture and text rights reserved for all
countries. No part of this publication may
be reproduced in any manner whatsoever.

All rights reserved.

While we strive for utmost precision in
every detail, we cannot be held responsible
for any inaccuracies, neither for any
subsequent loss or damage arising.

Bibliographic information published by
Die Deutsche Bibliothek.
Die Deutsche Bibliothek lists this publication
in the Deutsche Nationalbibliografie;
detailed bibliographic data is available
in the Internet at http://dnb.ddb.de

감사합니다

감사합니다

감사합니다

謝。謝。

謝。謝。

謝。謝。

謝。謝。

Cám ơn

Cám ơn

Cám ơn

Cám ơn.

It is now time to pay attention to Asia!

Although a long time has passed since Marco Polo or the early Christian missionaries visited the region, Asia, the world's largest continent, is still largely unknown to most Westerners. In this vast area, characterized by its great diversity in terms of geography, race, religion, language and tradition, an awareness of the various cultural identities in existence can only be achieved through understanding and inter-cultural communication. This variety of cultures in Asia has created a very diverse architecture. Nowadays, the swift pace of globalization and the advance of new technologies are taking many of these ancient cultures on a collision course between tradition and modernity. In this respect, Asian architecture should be understood as a powerful tool for shaping the future of the continent, while at the same time safeguarding its invaluable heritage. Asia is the Kanji (Chinese characters) culture of the countries in East Asia, the Hindu culture of the Indian subcontinent, the Islamic societies prevalent in South-East Asia; it is rapidly developing countries coexisting alongside highly industrialized nations, and it is also much more. It is therefore time to stop looking at Asia primarily in terms of exoticism, ethnicity, Orientalism, etc.

This book, which presents residential works created by a wide range of architects, stretching from India to Japan, provides the opportunity to become familiar with the realities of this fascinating continent. Despite obvious differences in their history and background, most Asian countries experienced periods of great growth in the 20th century, especially after World War II; this growth gave rise to a frantic drive to catch up with the modernization process, too often leading in its turn to a false Westernization in many cities, with the end result, in a great many cases, being an all-pervading chaos. These days, however, many talented Asian architects, such as Yung Ho Chang (China), Seung, H-Sang (South Korea), Kanika R'kul (Thailand) and Frank Ling (Malaysia), are trying to recover the best of Asian tradition while creating new prototypes for city planning and residential architecture. Many of these architects studied abroad and have therefore acquired a different perspective of their own countries. In order to better understand this awareness, there follow a few reflections from some of the architects featured in this book. Their words help give greater insight into the special characteristics of the region.

Vasant Kamath from Delhi, India, argues that *"From the heritage of the traditional, dense urban fabric of narrow, shady streets and internal courtyards, to the detached colonial bungalow with its lawns and gardens, post-independence residential architecture in India has lacked an appropriate framework. Dictated largely by antiquated building laws, the architecture of the house from the 50s onwards has mostly been constrained within a given framework of semi-detached and terraced houses in plotted layouts. Villas for the rich in suburban outskirts, apartment buildings in metropolitan cities and large housing projects for the poor or for institution, are some of the exceptions to this scenario. Stylistically, the expression of the house has evolved from Le Corbusier- and Khan-influenced modernism in the 1960s and 1970s, to an explosion of post-modern, historical revivalism in the 1980s and 1990s. The existence of a strong craft tradition and the Indian urge to decorate are finding expression in the elaborate, hand-crafted houses of today, vying for individual attention in an incoherent urban landscape."*

Seung, H-Sang from South Korea talks about Seoul, its capital city, *"in terms of a planned city that had been carefully designed following the fundamentals of Feng Shui. Even though it is considered to be a planned city, the "plan" consisted of just a few considerations regarding the optimal location and the road design for the castle grounds, its premises and the precinct. A hilly city located in the middle of the space created by four mountains that surround it to the North, South, East and West, this is considered an optimal location according to the rules of Feng Shui. As it is not built on a flat plain, the building method for Seoul could not develop in the same way as it did for cities such as Beijing or Tokyo. In these cities, building the roads came first and then came the division of the land to build fixed form-fitting residential dwellings. Instead, in Seoul residential areas were developed first along the foothills and along the rivers and the roads came later, using the area left-over from the residential dwellings. Basically, the road is not regarded as a function of a network but as a margin or void between houses. This is the reason why the roads have taken the shape of something similar to a complex maze.*

After the Korean War, a new materialistic culture based on America's value system has changed Korea's housing style. Especially from the 60s onwards, when rapid economic development was the prime national agenda of the government, Western style houses became the dream of Korean citizens. Their advent meant the progressive filling-up of the open courtyard space—or Madang—that was the centre of traditional Korean urban housing."

Seung, H-Sang's residential works are a counteroffensive to the contemporary houses produced during the course of this Westernization, an attempt to recapture the memories of the forgotten spiritual space, described by the architect as "forgotten emptiness".

Zhang Xin of Soho China, the promoters of "The Commune by The Great Wall" project, argues that *"China, after 50 years of Communism, is trans-*

forming and reinventing herself socially, economically and artistically. City planners are catching up with modernization plans; real estate developers are busy building "dream homes" for first-time home owners; architects are working day and night and still unable to reduce the queues for drawings outside their offices. The frantic level of energy and the huge amount of construction in such a short period of time has given China almost no time to search for her own contemporary architecture."

Soho China's great vision was to build a contemporary architectural museum comprising 12 private houses, designed by 12 Asian architects, in a valley measuring 3 sq. miles (8 sq. km), next to the Great Wall. According to Zhang Xin, *"with the aim of influencing a whole generation of architects, developers and consumers in China, they hope the project will contribute to the history of architecture in their re-born "young" country. Emphasizing the experimental spirit of "The Commune", the added flavor was that invitations to participate in the project were only given to Asian architects, 12 architects who symbolize the rise of development in Asia, particularly in China".*

"The Commune by The Great Wall" project reaped the rewards of Soho China's vision when it was invited to participate in the Venice Biennale and went on to win its special prize. Deyan Sudjic, the director of the Biennale, described the project as *"a combination of aesthetic ambition and the reinforcement of Asian identity through architectural innovation that contributes to the setting of the architectural agenda for this coming decade".* Kay Ngee Tan of Singapore thinks "the Commune project will be of great significance, changing the way the Chinese look at houses, architecture and spaces at present". According to Tan, *"the Commune must have set a standard for the architectural scene in China".*

As regards Japan, the book features the work of a number of well-known, emerging young architects like Shigeru Ban, Takaharu and Yui Tezuka, Akira Sakamoto, Kengo Kuma, etc. All these Japanese architects have an interna-

tional outlook and they are also exerting a positive influence on other Asian countries. Finally we would like to quote the words of Satoshi Asakawa, a Japanese photographer from Tokyo who specializes in Asian architecture. Without his much appreciated collaboration, the task of collecting architectural projects around Asia would have proved much more difficult.

"Almost ten years have passed since I started my journey in search of emerging architecture around Asia. Despite having been born in Japan, at the far end of the Far East, it had always been difficult for me to recognize myself as already being in Asia. I often wondered whether there would be a surprising land out there in the continent, full of dream stories waiting for me. However, such vain dreams did not exist out there, only the reality of the architectural works that I encountered. Still, I managed to occasionally catch the glimpse of a twinkling dream among the architects I met, in the beautiful nature I witnessed, in the chaotic yet friendly and charming crowd I mingled with; along the entire path of my Asian pilgrimage, some sort of dream was still there."

Although only a limited number of works have been included in this book, it is the aim of *Asian Interior Design* to allow its readers to acquire a closer understanding of the complexities and fascinating challenges involved in such a broad term as "Asia", through its architecture, which stands beside the best architecture being produced anywhere else in the world.

Die Zeit ist gekommen, den Blick auf Asien zu richten!

Obwohl Marco Polo und die christlichen Missionare schon vor langer Zeit Asien bereisten, ist der weltweit größte Kontinent den meisten Menschen der westlichen Hemisphäre bis heute noch unbekannt geblieben. In diesem gewaltigen Kontinent, der sich durch seine geographische, ethnische, religiöse, sprachliche und traditionelle Vielfalt auszeichnet, kann nur durch Einsicht und interkulturelle Kommunikation ein Bewusstsein der heutigen kulturellen Identitäten erreicht werden. Die Kulturvielfalt in Asien drückt sich auch in seiner unterschiedlichen Architektur aus. Durch das rasende Tempo der Globalisation und die Entwicklung neuer Technologien sind heutzutage viele alte Kulturen zwischen die Fronten von Modernität und Tradition geraten. In diesem Aspekt sollte die asiatische Architektur als ein machtvolles Werkzeug verstanden werden, mit dessen Hilfe die Zukunft des Kontinents entworfen wird, während gleichzeitig das unschätzbare Erbe bewahrt bleibt. Asien bedeutet die chinesische Kanjikultur der ostasiatischen Länder, die Hindukultur Vorderindiens, der in den südostasiatischen Ländern vorherrschende Islam; Asien bedeutet auch sich schnell entwickelnde Länder, die in Koexistenz mit hoch industrialisierten Ländern leben, und noch vieles mehr. Der Blick auf Asien sollte nicht durch Exotik, Orientalismus, Ethnologie etc. verstellt werden.

Die in diesem Buch vorgenommene Präsentation von Wohngebäuden, die von einer großen Anzahl verschiedener Architekten von Indien bis Japan entworfen wurde, soll eine Gelegenheit bieten, sich mit den Begebenheiten dieses faszinierenden Kontinents vertraut zu machen. Trotz evidenter historischer Unterschiede erlebten die meisten asiatischen Länder im 20. Jahrhundert, insbesondere nach dem 2. Weltkrieg, einen enormen wirtschaftlichen Aufschwung, der zu einem im rasenden Tempo vollzogenen Modernisierungsprozess führte. Leider wurde Modernisierung in vielen Fällen mit einer falschen Verwestlichung verwechselt, deren Ergebnis heute in vielen Städten als ein alles durchdringendes Chaos zu bestaunen ist. Heutzutage aber unternehmen viele talentierte Architekten, wie Yung Ho Chang (China), Seung, H-Sang (Südkorea), Kanika R'kul (Thailand) und

Frank Ling (Malaysia), den Versuch, die Essenz asiatischer Kultur wiederherzustellen und auf Städte- und Häuserbau anzuwenden. Viele dieser
Architekten studierten im Ausland, und konnten so ihre Heimatländer in
einer neuen Perspektive betrachten. Zum besseren Verständnis dieses
Bewusstseins sollen im Folgenden ein paar Überlegungen von einigen im
Buch vorgestellten Architekten zitiert werden. Durch ihre Äußerungen erhalten wir einen tieferen Einblick in die speziellen Eigenschaften ihrer Heimat.

Vasant Kamath aus dem indischen Delhi räsoniert: *„Von dem Erbe des traditionellen, dichten städtischen Gefüge mit engen, schattigen Straßen und
Innenhöfen bis zu dem kolonialen Bungalow mit seinen Rasenflächen und
Gärten fehlte der Wohnarchitektur im unabhängigen Indien immer ein
eigenständiges Rahmenkonzept. Durch antiquierte Bauverordnungen fest-
gelegt, beschränkt sich die Wohnhausarchitektur seit den 50er Jahren in
erster Linie auf Doppel- oder Reihenhäuser auf abgesteckten Grundstücken,
wobei am Stadtrand gelegene Villen für die Reichen, Apartmenthäuser in
Großstädten und umfangreiche Wohnprojekte für die Armen oder institu-
tionelle Einrichtungen die Ausnahme bilden. Stilistisch hat sich die
Architektur von einem an Le Corbusier und Khan angelehnten Modernismus
in den 1960er und 1970er Jahren zu einer postmodernen historischen
Erneuerung in den 1980er und 1990er Jahren entwickelt. Eine starke
Handwerkstradition und das indische Bedürfnis nach Dekoration findet
heutzutage in den handwerklich ausgefeilten Häusern seinen Ausdruck, die
in einer inkohärenten Stadtlandschaft die Aufmerksamkeit Vorbeieilender
auf sich ziehen."*

Seung, H-Sang aus Südkorea schreibt über Seoul, dass diese Hauptstadt *„sehr vorsichtig nach den Grundsätzen des Feng Shui angelegt wurde. Obwohl als geplante Stadt angesehen, bestand die Planung lediglich aus der optimalen Standortbestimmung und dem Straßenentwurf für die Schlossanlage, sein Anwesen und seine Umgebung. Nach den Regeln des Feng Shui besitzt Seoul als eine hügelige Stadt, die in nördlicher, südlicher, östlicher und westlicher Richtung von vier Bergen umgeben ist, einen optimalen Standort. Da nicht auf ebener Fläche gebaut wurde, hat sich hier eine zu Städten wie Peking oder Tokio unterschiedliche Baumethode entwickelt. Während in diesen Städten zunächst die Straßen angelegt wurden, und danach das Land eingeteilt und mit fertig genormten Wohnhäusern bebaut wurde, waren es in Seoul zunächst die Wohngebiete, die im Vorgebirge und entlang der Flüsse entstanden, wobei die Straßen erst später aus den unbebauten Zwischenräumen hervorgingen. Die Straße im Allgemeinen besitzt hier keine verbindende Funktion, sondern wird eher als Grenze oder Leerraum zwischen den Häusern empfunden. Aus diesem Grunde erinnern die Straßen in ihrer Form an Labyrinthe.*

Nach dem Korea-Krieg veränderte eine materialistische an Amerikas Wertesystem angelehnte Kultur Koreas Wohnstil. Mit dem von der Regierung als absolute Priorität angestrebten wirtschaftlichen Aufschwung erlangten die Häuser im westlichen Stil besonders ab den 60ern ungeheure Beliebtheit, was mit dem zunehmenden Ausfüllen des offenen Innenhofes – oder Madang – dem Zentrum des traditionellen Stadthauses, einherging."

Die von Seung, H-Sang erbauten Wohnhäuser bilden eine Gegenoffensive zu den im Zuge der Verwestlichung produzierten zeitgenössischen Häusern und stellen den Versuch dar, sich den in Vergessenheit geratenen spirituellen Raum, vom Architekten „vergessene Leere" genannt, erneut in Erinnerung zu rufen.

Der Bauträger des Projekts „The Commune by The Great Wall" Zhang Xin von Soho China, argumentiert, dass *„China sich heute nach 50 Jahren*

Bangladesh

Kommunismus im Prozess der sozialen, wirtschaftlichen und künstlerischen Umwandlung und Erneuerung befindet. Stadtplaner holen Modernisierungspläne ein und sind damit beschäftigt, „Traumhäuser" für erstmalige Hausbesitzer zu bauen, während Architekten Tag und Nacht arbeiten, ohne dass sich der Ansturm auf ihre Büros verringert. Das äußerst hohe Maß an Betriebsamkeit und die große Anzahl neuer Gebäude in kürzester Zeit haben dazu geführt, dass China kaum Zeit hat, eine eigene aktuelle Architektur zu entwickeln."

Der Bau eines zeitgenössischen Architekturmuseums, bestehend aus 12 von 12 asiatischen Architekten entworfenen Wohnhäusern, die in einem 8 km² großen Tal in der Nähe der Chinesischen Mauer erbaut wurden, war Soho Chinas große Vision. Laut Zhang Xin „war es das Ziel, eine ganze Generation von chinesischen Architekten, Stadtplanern und Konsumenten mit diesem Projekt zu beeinflussen und einen Beitrag zur Architekturgeschichte in ihrem neugeborenen „jungen" Land zu leisten. Um den experimentellen Charakter der „Commune" hervorzuheben, wurden nur asiatische Architekten zu diesem Projekt eingeladen, 12 Architekten, die den Aufschwung in Asien, besonders in China symbolisieren."

Das Projekt „The Commune by The Great Wall" erntete mit Soho Chinas Vision großen Beifall, indem es zu der Teilnahme an der Biennale in Venedig eingeladen und dort mit einem besonderen Preis ausgezeichnet wurde. Der Direktor der Biennale, Deyan Sudjic, beschieb das Projekt als „eine Kombination aus ästhetischer Ambition und der Stärkung asiatischer Identität durch architektonische Innovation, welche richtungsweisend für die architektonische Agenda der kommenden Dekade ist". Kay Ngee Tan aus Singapur denkt, dass „das Commune-Projekt von großer Bedeutung ist und die Betrachtungsweise der Chinesen im Hinblick auf Häuser, Architektur und Raum verändern wird". Laut Tan „hat the Commune in China einen Standard für die architektonische Szene geschaffen".

Im Hinblick auf Japan stellt dieses Buch eine Anzahl bekannter junger Architekten vor, wie Shigeru Ban, Takaharu und Yui Tezuka, Akira Sakamoto, Kengo Kuma, etc. All diese japanischen Architekten haben internationales Ansehen und üben einen positiven Einfluss auf die anderen asiatischen Länder aus. Zum Schluss soll der in asiatischer Architektur spezialisierte Fotograf Satoshi Asakawa aus Tokio zitiert werden, ohne dessen geschätzte Hilfe das Zusammentragen architektonischer Projekte in Asien weitaus schwieriger verlaufen wäre:

„Vor fast zehn Jahren begann meine Suche nach Architektur in Asien. Obwohl ich in Japan geboren bin, am fernen Ende vom fernen Osten, fiel es mir immer schwer, mich als ein in Asien lebender Mensch zu begreifen. Oft fragte ich mich, ob nicht irgendwo in diesem Kontinent ein Zauberland mit Traumgeschichten auf mich wartete. Dennoch waren es nicht diese Träume, sondern die Realität der architektonischen Arbeiten, auf die ich stieß. Und doch gelang es mir manchmal, einen flüchtigen Blick auf einen glänzenden Traum bei den Architekten, die ich traf, zu erhaschen, in der schönen Natur, die ich erfuhr, in der chaotischen und doch freundlichen und charmanten Menschenmenge, unter die ich mich mischte; während des gesamten Weges meiner asiatischen Pilgerfahrt waren einige Träume noch vorhanden."

In dem Bewusstsein, dass in diesem Buch nur eine begrenzte Anzahl von Arbeiten vorgestellt werden kann, ist es doch das Ziel mit *Asian Interior Design* den Lesern via Architektur, die der besten Architektur überall in der Welt in nichts nachsteht, einen näheren Einblick in die Komplexität und die faszinierenden Herausforderungen, die der weite Begriff „Asien" beinhaltet, zu gestatten und ein größeres Verständnis dafür zu erzeugen.

L'heure est venue de porter le regard vers l'Asie!

Bien que le temps ait passé depuis Marco Polo et la visite des premiers missionnaires chrétiens dans la région, l'Asie, le plus vaste des continents, demeure immensément inconnue de la plupart des occidentaux. Dans un territoire gigantesque, caractérisé par sa grande diversité en termes de géographie, race, religion, langage et de tradition, la conscience des diverses identités culturelles naît uniquement de la compréhension et de la communication interculturelle. Cette variété de cultures en Asie a créé une architecture très diversifiée. De nos jours, la marche forcée de la globalisation et l'avance des nouvelles technologies mènent ces cultures antiques sur la voie de la collision entre tradition et modernité. Dans cette optique, l'architecture asiatique doit être comprise comme un outil puissant permettant de donner forme au futur du continent tout en préservant son héritage si précieux. L'Asie est la culture des Kanji (caractères chinois) des pays de ﬁlture hindoue du sous-continent indien, la prévalence ﬁues du Sud-est asiatique, des pays en développement ﬁavec des nations hautement industrialisées et bien plus ﬁmps de cesser d'appréhender l'Asie en termes d'exotis- ﬁientalisme, etc.

présente les intérieurs domestiques créés par tout un ﬁs, de l'Inde au Japon, offre l'opportunité de se familia- ﬁs de ce continent fascinant. En dépit de différences évi- ﬁde contexte, la plupart des pays ont connu des périodes ﬁance au 20ème siècle, spécialement après la Seconde ﬁtte croissance a donné lieu à une course effrénée pour progrès, menant plus qu'à son tour à une occidentali- ﬁombre de cités avec pour résultat final, le plus souvent, ﬁnt. Ces derniers temps, cependant, une pléthore d'ar- ﬁde talent, ainsi Yung Ho Chang (Chine), Seung, H-Sang ﬁika R'kul (Thaïlande) et Frank Ling (Malaisie), tentent de ﬁde la tradition de l'Asie tout en donnant vie à de nou- ﬁle planification urbaine et d'architecture résidentiel. ﬁitectes ont étudié à l'étranger et ont donc acquis une perspective différente de leur propre pays. Afin de mieux comprendre cette prise conscience, voici quelques réflexions de certains des architectes présentés dans cet ouvrage. Leurs mots offrent une perception plus intense des caractéristiques spécifiques de la région.

Vasant Kamath de Delhi, en Inde, avance : « *De l'héritage d'un tissu urbain traditionnel dense aux rues étroites et ombragées et de cours intérieures jusqu'aux bungalows coloniaux arborant jardins et pelouses, l'architecture résidentielle post-indépendance en Inde a manqué de cadre de travail approprié. Largement dictée par des règles de construction antiques, l'architecture de la maison à partir des années 1950 a essentiellement été confinée à un programme imposé de maisons adossées en terrasse, selon des dispositions précises. Les villas des riches en périphérie des villes, les immeubles d'appartements des grandes métropoles et les projets de HLM pour les plus pauvres ou les institutions se trouvent parmi les exceptions qui confirment la règle. Sur le plan stylistique, l'expression de la maison a évolué depuis Le Corbusier- et Khan-modernisme sous influen-*

ce dans les années 1960 et 1970 jusqu'à l'explosion de l'esprit du renouveau historique et post-moderne des années 1980 et 1990. L'existence d'un solide savoir-faire traditionnel et le besoin indien d'ornementation trouvent leur expression dans les demeures contemporaines, élaborées et personnalisées, rivalisant pour attirer l'attention dans un paysage urbain incohérent. »

Seung, H-Sang, de Corée du sud, parle de Séoul, sa capitale, « *en termes de cité planifiée, pensée avec attention afin de respecter les principes fondamentaux du Feng Shui. Même si elle est considérée comme une ville planifiée, le « plan » a essentiellement* consisté en quelques considérations relatives à l'emplacement idéal et la conception routière pour les terres du château, ses prémisses et les alentours. Une cité vallonnée au cœur d'un espace créé par quatre montagnes l'encadrant au Nord, Sud, Est et Ouest : un emplacement optimal selon les règles du Feng Shui. Comme elle n'est pas construite sur une plaine, les méthodes de construction pour Séoul n'ont pu se développer comme ce fut le cas pour des cités comme Beijing ou Tokyo. Pour ces villes, l'établissement des routes s'est d'abord imposé suivi de la division des terrains afin d'ériger des demeures résidentielles aux formes définies. En revanche, les quartiers résidentiels de Séoul ont d'abord été développés le long des collines et rivières pour voir, ensuite, arriver les routes, sur les terrains demeurés inoccupés par les maisons. Fondamentalement, la route n'est pas perçue comme une fonction d'un réseau mais comme une marge, un vide entre les maisons. C'est pourquoi les routes ont adopté une forme similaire à celle d'un labyrinthe complexe.

Après la guerre de Corée, une nouvelle culture matérialiste reposant sur le système de valeurs des États-Unis a modifié le style des logements coréens. Plus spécifiquement à compter des années 60, lorsque le pas rapide du développement économique était le point principal de l'ordre du jour du gouvernement, les maisons à l'occidentale sont devenues le rêve des citoyens coréens. Leur avènement signifiait le remplissage progressif de l'espace des cours ouvertes – ou Madang – au centre du logement urbain coréen traditionnelle. »

Les travaux résidentiels de Seung, H-Sang sont une contre-offensive envers les maisons contemporaines produites lors de ce mouvement d'occidentalisation, une tentative visant à recouvrer la mémoire de cette espace spirituel oublié, décrit par l'architecte comme « un vide oublié ».

Zhang Xin de Soho China, les promoteurs du projet « The Commune by The Great Wall », déclare que « La Chine, après 50 ans de communisme, se transforme et se réinvente socialement, économiquement et artistiquement. Les

Indonesia

urbanistes se remettent dans le bain des plans de modernisation ; les promoteurs immobiliers sont occupés à construire des « maisons de rêve » pour les nouveaux propriétaires ; les architectes travaillent nuit et jour tout en demeurant incapables de réduire les files d'attente pour des plans devant leurs cabinets. La frénésie d'énergie et la pléthore de travaux de construction en un temps si court n'ont pratiquement pas laissé de temps à la Chine pour effectuer des recherches pour sa propre architecture contemporaine ».

La grande vision de Soho China portait sur la construction d'un musée architectural contemporain comprenant 12 maisons privées, conçues par 12 architectes asiatiques, dans une vallée de 8 km², à proximité de la Grande Muraille. Selon Zhang Xin, « avec pour objectif d'influencer toute une génération d'architectes, de développeurs et de consommateurs en Chine, ils espèrent que le projet pourra contribuer à l'histoire de l'architecture dans un « jeune » pays en renaissance. Rehaussant l'esprit expérimental de « The Commune », une touche supplémentaire a conduit à inviter à participer au projet uniquement des architectes asiatiques, 12 architectes symbolisant la montée du développement en Asie, particulièrement en Chine ».

Le projet « The Commune by The Great Wall » a recueilli les fruits des efforts de la vision de Soho China après avoir été invité à participer à la Biennale de Venise, pour remporter son prix spécial. Deyan Sudjic, le directeur de la Biennale, a décrit le projet comme « une combinaison d'ambition esthétique et de renforcement de l'identité asiatique grâce à l'innovation architecturale, contribuant à établir un calendrier pour la prochaine décennie ». Kay Ngee Tan, de Singapour, pense que « le projet Commune sera extrêmement significatif, changeant la façon dont les Chinois regardent leurs maisons, leur architecture et leurs espaces aujourd'hui ». Selon Tan, « le projet Commune constitue désormais un standard pour la scène architecturale en Chine ».

Quant au Japon, le livre présente les œuvres de nombreux jeunes architectes, émergents et reconnus, ainsi Shigeru Ban, Takaharu et Yui Tezuka,

Akira Sakamoto, Kengo Kuma, etc. Tous ces créateurs japonais bénéficient d'une vision internationale et exercent également une influence positive sur les autres pays asiatiques. Enfin, il faut citer les paroles de Satoshi Asakawa, un photographe japonais de Tokyo, spécialisé en architecture asiatique. Sans sa participation, à laquelle nous sommes hautement sensibles, la tâche visant à collecter les projets architecturaux dans l'ensemble de l'Asie se serait révélée bien plus ardue.

« Près de dix ans se sont écoulés depuis que j'ai commencé mon voyage en quête de l'architecture naissante à travers l'Asie. Bien que né au japon, à l'extrême de l'Extrême Orient, j'ai toujours éprouvé une certaine difficulté à me reconnaître comme présent en Asie. Je me suis souvent demandé s'il se trouverait une contrée surprenante, quelque part sur le continent, aux histoires oniriques, n'attendant que moi. Quoi qu'il en soit, ces rêves de vanité n'existent pas ici bas, seule la réalité des œuvres architecturales que j'ai rencontré. Pourtant, j'ai pu, occasionnellement, saisir quelques visions fugitives d'étincelles de rêves avec les architectes que j'ai connu, au cœur de la nature dont j'ai été le spectateur, parmi la foule chaotique mais aussi amicale et envoûtante à laquelle je me suis mêlé, tout au long du cheminement de mon pèlerinage asiatique. Le souvenir du rêve était demeuré présent. »

Bien que nous soyons parfaitement conscients que ce livre nous ait seulement laissé inclure un nombre limité d'œuvres, nous serions cependant satisfaits si *Asian Interior Design* permettait à ses lecteurs d'acquérir un entendement plus intime des complexités et des défis fascinants impliqués par un mot aussi vaste que « Asie », grâce à son architecture, l'égale de la meilleure architecture produite où que ce soit dans le reste du monde.

¡Es hora de dirigir la mirada hacia Asia!

Aunque ha pasado ya mucho tiempo desde la época en que Marco Polo o los antiguos misioneros cristianos visitaron esta región, Asia, a pesar de ocupar el continente más extenso del planeta, continúa siendo, en gran medida, una área desconocida para la mayor parte del mundo occidental. En este inmenso territorio caracterizado por su gran diversidad geográfica, de etnias, religiones, lenguas y tradiciones, solamente mediante el entendimiento y la comunicación intercultural se puede tener conciencia de las diversas identidades culturales que se dan cita. En Asia, la gran variedad de culturas ha protagonizado una arquitectura muy diversa. En la actualidad, el ritmo trepidante de la globalización, junto con el avance de las nuevas tecnologías, hace que estas antiguas culturas se encaminen hacia un proceso de confrontación entre tradición y modernidad. En este sentido, la arquitectura de Asia tendría que entenderse como un instrumento determinante para forjar el futuro del continente, al tiempo que contribuye a la salvaguarda de su valioso patrimonio cultural. Asia es la cultura kanji (carácteres chinos) de los países que conforman el este del continente, la cultura hindú del subcontinente indio, las sociedades islámicas preponderantes en los países del sudeste asiático; es también un gran número de países emergentes que coexisten con otros sumamente industrializados... y mucho más. Ya va siendo hora, por tanto, de dejar de mirar a Asia en clave de exotismo, identidad étnica, orientalismo, etcétera.

Este libro, mediante la obra creada por un amplio abanico de arquitectos que engloba desde India hasta Japón, presenta al lector la oportunidad de familiarizarse con la realidad de este fascinante continente. A pesar de evidentes diferencias en cuanto a historia y antecedentes, la mayoría de los países asiáticos experimentaron durante el siglo XX, especialmente después de la Segunda Guerra Mundial, periodos de gran crecimiento económico. Este crecimiento dio lugar a un frenético dinamismo para alcanzar un proceso de modernización que en muchos casos dio como resultado una falsa occidentalización de las ciudades y, en mayor medida, un caos generalizado en estos núcleos. Hoy en día, sin embargo, muchos arquitectos asiáticos de talento como Yung Ho Chang (China), Seung, H-Sang (Corea del Sur),

Kanika R'kul (Tailandia) o Frank Ling (Malasia) están intentando recuperar lo mejor de la tradición asiática, creando al mismo tiempo nuevos prototipos en urbanismo y arquitectura residencial. Muchos de ellos estudiaron en su momento en el extranjero, donde tuvieron la oportunidad de adquirir una perspectiva distinta de la de su propio país. Con el fin de mejorar la comprensión de su concienciación, he aquí ciertas reflexiones de algunos de los arquitectos presentes en el libro. Sus palabras ayudarán al lector a conocer las peculiares características de la región.

Vasant Kamath, natural de Delhi, India, sostiene que "*ya sea desde nuestro tradicional y denso patrimonio urbano, compuesto por patios interiores y estrechas y turbias callejuelas, ya desde el clásico bungalow colonial con césped y jardines, la arquitectura residencial de India ha adolecido de la falta de un marco concreto apropiado. Dependiente de obsoletas reglamentaciones en materia de construcción, la arquitectura residencial levantada a partir de los años cincuenta se ha limitado a hileras de casas uniformes o a viviendas semiadosadas en determinados trazados. Algunas excepciones a este panorama las encontramos en los chalés de gente adinerada construidos en las afueras de las grandes ciudades, en los edificios de apartamentos de las metrópolis y en los grandes bloques de pisos erigidos para los menos favorecidos o para instituciones. Estilísticamente, el semblante de la casa ha evolucionado desde el modernismo de los años sesenta y setenta, influenciado por Le Corbusier y Khan, hasta la eclosión de un renacer histórico y posmoderno durante los años ochenta y noventa. La existencia de una marcada tradición artesanal, junto con la necesidad imperiosa india de recurrir a la decoración, encuentran su más viva expresión en las elaboradas viviendas artesanales de hoy en día, que compiten para llamar la atención en medio de un incoherente paisajismo urbano.*"

Seung, H-Sang, de Corea del Sur, habla de la capital de su país, Seúl, "*como una ciudad que ha sido cuidadosamente proyectada siguiendo los fundamentos del feng shui. Aun cuando se considera una ciudad planificada, esta planificación consiste tan solo en unas meras consideracio-*

nes con respecto a la óptima ubicación y al entramado de calles, de las tierras circundantes al palacio, el recinto que lo delimita y a sus edificios. La ubicación de la ciudad, con un terreno empinado y rodeada por cuatro montañas en los cuatro puntos cardinales, es considerada ideal según los principios del feng shui. Al no estar posada sobre terreno plano, la metodología de construcción de Seúl no siguió las pautas de ciudades como Tokio o Pekín. En estas metrópolis, antes de la partición y distribución de la tierra para la construcción de viviendas se efectuó la planificación y posterior construcción de su entramado de calles, al contrario que en Seúl, en donde se priorizó la arquitectura residencial en las estribaciones de las colinas y en las orillas de los ríos. Las calles, que aparecieron posteriormente, se trazaron en los espacios sobrantes entre viviendas. Fundamentalmente, no se considera que la calle tenga una función dentro de un sistema, sino que es más bien un espacio vacío entre casas. Ésta es la razón por la cual la red de calles y carreteras ha adoptado la forma de un complejo laberinto.

"Una vez acabada la guerra de Corea, aparece en el país un nuevo estilo de vivienda producto de una nueva cultura materialista que se alimenta del sistema de valores estadounidense. En particular, es a partir de la década de los sesenta cuando, gracias al rápido despegue económico propulsado por el gobierno del país, la vivienda al estilo occidental se convierte en el sueño del ciudadano coreano. La llegada de este tipo de vivienda supone, por otra parte, el final del clásico patio interior —o madang— alrededor del cual se construía la vivienda tradicional coreana."

La arquitectura residencial de Seung, H-Sang representa una contraofensiva al estilo de vivienda creado durante el periodo marcado por el proceso de occidentalización del país. Es un intento de recuperar la memoria de un espacio espiritual olvidado, descrito por el arquitecto como vacío olvidado.

Zhang Xin, directora de Soho China, empresa promotora del proyecto denominado The Commune by The Great Wall (La comuna junto a la Gran

Muralla), argumenta que *"China, después de 50 años de comunismo, se está transformando y reinventando tanto a escala social, como económica y artística. Urbanistas absortos en proyectos de modernización; promotores inmobiliarios ocupados en construir 'casas de ensueño' para sus futuros y nuevos propietarios; arquitectos que trabajando día y noche ven sus talleres desbordados por la demanda de proyectos. El enfervorizado nivel de energía y el alto índice de construcción que se está registrando en China en un periodo de tiempo tan reducido hacen que el país no haya podido aún ir a la búsqueda de su verdadera arquitectura contemporánea."*

La amplitud de miras de Soho China se tradujo en su visión para construir un museo de arquitectura que consta de 12 chalets privados, diseñados por otros tantos arquitectos asiáticos, en un valle de 8 km² situado junto a la Gran Muralla. Según Zhang Xin, *"con el propósito de influenciar a toda una generación de arquitectos, promotores y consumidores en China, desean que el proyecto sirva para contribuir a la historia de la arquitectura de su 'renacido' país. Haciendo hincapié en el carácter experimental de la comuna, destacaría como factor adicional el hecho de que las invitaciones para participar en el proyecto fueran sólo a arquitectos asiáticos, 12 arquitectos que simbolizan el creciente desarrollo de Asia, y de China en particular."*

El proyecto de "The Commune by The Great Wall" cosechó los frutos visionarios de Soho China al ser invitado a participar en la Bienal de Venecia y hacerse con el premio especial del certamen. Deyan Sudjic, director de la Bienal, describió el proyecto como *"la combinación de una ambición estética y el refuerzo de una identidad asiática mediante la innovación arquitectónica, que marcará el orden del día de la arquitectura durante esta próxima década"*. Kay Ngee Tan, de Singapur, cree que *"el proyecto de la comuna tendrá una gran significación y provocará un cambio en la manera como los ciudadanos chinos contemplan las casas, la arquitectura y los espacios en la actualidad"*. Según Tan, *"la comuna debería establecer el nivel del panorama arquitectónico en China"*.

En cuanto a Japón, el libro muestra los trabajos de un buen número de incipientes jóvenes arquitectos como Shigeru Ban, Takaharu y Yui Tezuka, Akira Sakamoto, Kengo Kuma, etcétera. Todos ellos tienen una amplitud de miras internacional y están también ejerciendo una influencia positiva en otros países de Asia. Finalmente, hay que citar las palabras de Satoshi Asakawa, un fotógrafo japonés natural de Tokio especializado en arquitectura de Asia. Sin su estimada colaboración, la tarea de recopilación de proyectos por todo el continente asiático habría sido una empresa mucho más ardua.

"Han pasado ya casi diez años desde que me embarqué en un viaje en búsqueda de la arquitectura joven y emergente de Asia. A pesar de haber nacido en Japón, en los confines del Extremo Oriente, siempre me resultó difícil reconocerme como un ser que habitaba ya en Asia. A menudo me preguntaba si por allá, en el continente, habría un mundo lleno de sorpresas, repleto de historias de ensueño esperando mi llegada. Sin embargo, dichos sueños vanos nunca existieron, sólo la realidad de la obra arquitectónica que iba encontrando al paso. Aun así, pude en ocasiones captar un centelleante sueño entre los arquitectos que conocí, en la maravillosa naturaleza que presencié, entre la caótica aunque encantadora muchedumbre con la que me mezclé; durante todo el sendero de mi peregrinaje por Asia, seguro que me acompañaba algún tipo de sueño."

Aunque tan solo un número limitado de obras han sido incluidas en este libro, el objetivo de *Asian Interior Design* es proporcionar entre los lectores un mayor entendimiento, mediante la arquitectura, de la complejidad y los fascinantes desafíos que un término tan amplio como Asia implica, una arquitectura que puede codearse perfectamente con lo mejor que se está produciendo en otras partes del planeta.

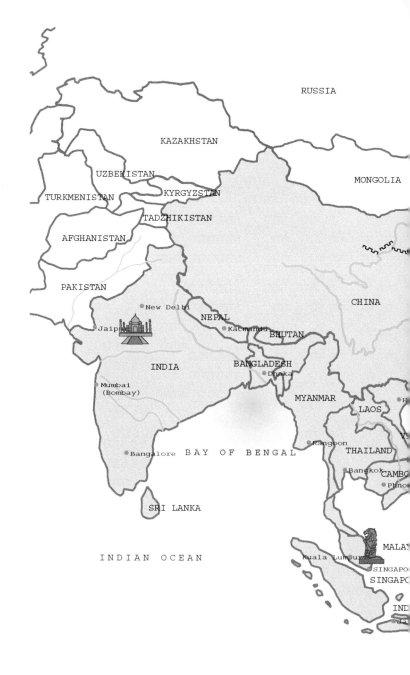

illustration: Tomoko Ihara

Architects: **Kashef Mahbood Chowdhury, Marina Tabassum**

Location: **Dhaka – Bangladesh**

Architects' Residence

Photographer: **Kashef / URBANA**   Completion date: **2002**

The architects used this opportunity to design their own home to explore the essence of their philosophy and existence in the creative process. The residence, on the sixth and uppermost floor of an apartment building that they themselves designed, was conceived as a large "pavilion in the air", left open to revel in the delights of the rain, sun and, on occasions, the tropical breezes. In this project, almost all the living area overlooks the courtyard, and when the glass shutters are moved to one side the space turns into a veranda. The dining/kitchen area is organized like an inner courtyard, with seating—both permanent and mobile—set around the edges. This makes it a perfect space for relaxed conversations with friends or relatives, following the Bengali tradition known as adda.

Bei dem Entwurf ihrer eigenen Wohnstätte nutzten die Architekten die Gelegenheit, sich mit der Essenz ihrer Lebensphilosophie auseinanderzusetzen. Die im sechsten, obersten Stockwerk eines Apartmenthauses gelegene Wohnung wurde als ein „Pavillon in der Luft" erdacht, dessen großzügige Offenheit es ermöglicht, den Regen, die Sonne und die seltene tropische Brise zu genießen. Fast das gesamte Wohnzimmer überblickt den Innenhof, und er verwandelt sich in eine Veranda, wenn die gläsernen Fensterläden auf eine Seite geschoben werden. Die wie ein Patio angelegte Küche/Essecke hat an den Seiten fest installierte oder bewegliche Sitzgelegenheiten. Es ist der ideale Ort für entspannte Unterhaltungen mit Freunden oder der Familie, in der bengalischen Tradition adda genannt.

Pour les architectes, la chance de concevoir leur propre résidence leur a permis d'explorer ainsi l'essence de leur propre philosophie de la vie. La demeure conçue, au sixième et dernier étage d'un immeuble d'appartements, a été pensée comme un « pavillon aérien », généreusement ouvert pour fêter les délices de la pluie, du soleil et de la brise tropicale, si rare. Pour ce projet, le séjour surplombe la cour et, en déplaçant les baies vitrées d'un côté, la chambre se fait véranda. L'aire repas/cuisine s'organise comme une cour intérieure, les sièges, permanents ou meubles, en périphérie. L'espace devient ensuite plus intime, pour des conversations paisibles avec la famille et les amis, la tradition bengali de l'adda.

La posibilidad de proyectar su propia residencia permitió a los arquitectos explorar la esencia de su filosofía y de su existencia. La vivienda, situada en el sexto y último piso de un edificio de apartamentos diseñado por ellos mismos, se concibió como un pabellón en el aire de amplias proporciones, gracias a las cuales sus residentes pueden deleitarse con los placeres de la lluvia, el sol y la ocasional brisa tropical. En este proyecto casi toda el área del salón domina el patio, que se convierte en una galería al apartar los postigos de cristal a un lado. La zona del comedor y la cocina está estructurada como un patio interior, con asientos –fijos o móviles– en su periferia. Esto hace de él un espacio ideal para conversaciones relajadas con amigos o parientes, siguiendo la tradición bengalí conocida como "adda".

45

Architects: **Kashef Mahbood Chowdhury, Marina Tabassum**

Location: **Dhaka – Bangladesh**

House at NEK 10

Photographer: **Kashef / URBANA** Completion date: **2001**

This house was designed for three brothers. One of them spends a lot of time abroad and so only requires a small apartment on the ground floor, while the other two have larger but similar apartments. In the front, steps typical of a "ghat"—a traditional river mooring—lead down to the lawn, which provides a space for relaxing and enjoying the garden in the cool evenings. Upstairs, the eating and family areas give on to terraces through the large windows on the south side, while the living space and staircase face the front. As the west-facing plot needed protection from the afternoon sun as well as privacy from the noise and bustle of the street, a spacious veranda was built to form a barrier. Here, the narrow windows offers glimpses of the garden while also allowing reflected light to penetrate into the interior.

Dieses Haus wurde für drei Brüder entworfen, von denen einer wegen häufiger Auslandsaufenthalte nur ein kleines Apartment im Parterre benötigt, während die beiden anderen die größeren, doch ähnlichen Wohnungen bevorzugen. Auf der Vorderseite des Hauses führen die Stufen eines "ghat"– der traditionellen Flussvertäuung entnommen – zum Rasen hinunter, wo sich die Bewohner an kühlen Abenden entspannen und den Garten genießen können. Im oberen Teil des Hauses blickt man von den Ess- und Familienräumen durch große Fenster auf die südlich gelegenen Terrassen, während der Wohnraum und das Treppenhaus nach vorne zeigen. Eine Veranda schützt die Westseite des Hauses vor der Nachmittagssonne und dem Lärm und Treiben der Straße. Gleichzeitig bieten schmale Fenster flüchtige Blicke in den Garten und lassen reflektiertes Sonnenlicht in das Haus hinein.

Cette maison est pensée pour trois frères, l'un souvent à l'étranger et nécessitant donc un petit logement en bas, les deux autres niveaux supérieurs étant plus grands bien que similaires. Devant, des marches de « ghat » – des amarres traditionnelles – descendent vers la pelouse, offrant un lieu de détente et où jouir du jardin. En haut, les espaces famille et repas donnent sur des terrasses au sud par de vastes ouvertures, séjour et escaliers regardant la façade. La parcelle ouest requérant une protection solaire l'après-midi mais aussi une intimité contre la circulation de la rue, une véranda en forme de vaste brise soleil et d'étroites ouvertures offrent des vues obliques du jardin, laissant entrer la lumière réfléchie à l'intérieur.

Esta casa se diseñó para tres hermanos, uno de los cuales residía con frecuencia en el extranjero y requería sólo un pequeño apartamento en la planta baja; las dos viviendas restantes, aunque similares, son más espaciosas. En la parte delantera, unos escalones tipo "ghat" –atracaderos típicamente fluviales– descienden sobre el césped y brindan a sus inquilinos un espacio para el relax en el jardín con el frescor de la tarde. Arriba, los espacios reservados a comedor y a la familia dan a terrazas en la cara sur gracias a generosos ventanales, mientras que el salón y las escaleras están orientados hacia la fachada. Para resguardarla del sol de la tarde y protegerla de los ruidos y el ajetreo de la calle, los arquitectos construyeron en la parte oeste una gran galería cubierta. Estrechas ventanas ofrecen asimismo vistas indirectas del jardín al tiempo que permiten la entrada de reflejos de luz en el interior.

Architects: **Revathi & Vasant Kamath**

Location: **Village Anangpur, Surajkund, Haryana – India**

Kamath House

Photographer: **Ram Rahman** Completion date: 1996

According to the architects, the relationship between the human habitat and nature has always been marked by exploitation. The spot on which their own house is situated provides a good illustration: here quarries have been dug to extract rock and stone, the forest cover has been chopped down for fire wood, etc. The Kamath House is an attempt to heal the wounds inflicted on the earth and establish a niche in the eco-system by regenerating the vegetation and creating a space and visual style based on the rearrangement of materials found on the grounds, on architecture that celebrates and nurtures the characteristics of natural elements. Kamath House embodies a lifestyle in which the human patterns within nature are constantly evolving.

Nach den Architekten wurde das Verhältnis zwischen menschlicher Existenz und Natur stets von Ausbeutung gekennzeichnet. Auch das Gelände ihres Hauses weist Spuren davon auf, sei es die durch das Heraushauen von Steinen aufgerissene Erde oder der für Brennholz entforstete Wald etc. Mit Kamath's House wird versucht, die offenen Wunden zu heilen und eine Nische im Öko-System zu errichten, in der sich das Grün ringsherum regenerieren kann. Architektur bedeutet hier das Erschaffen von Raum und Ästhetik durch eine Neubearbeitung der sich auf und um das Baugelände herum befindlichen Materialien, und auch, die Natur zu achten und zu bewahren. Kamath House repräsentiert einen Ort, in dem sich die menschliche Lebensweise innerhalb der Natur stetig entwickelt.

Selon les architectes, la relation de l'habitat humain à la nature a toujours reposé sur l'exploitation. Le site accueillant leur maison en est aussi un exemple, la terre ayant été creusée pour sa pierre, la forêt coupée pour son bois de chauffage, etc. Kamath's House est une tentative pour guérir la terre et nicher un écosystème susceptible de régénérer la forêt sur le site et pour laquelle l'architecture est une redistribution de matériaux, ça et là, pour créer espace et esthétisme. Une architecture selon laquelle les qualités vitales des éléments sont célébrées et nourries. Kamath House est un espace où l'évolution continue des modèles humains au sein de la nature est devenu un mode de vie.

Según estos arquitectos, la relación entre hábitat humano y naturaleza ha estado siempre marcada por la explotación que ha ejercido el hombre en su entorno. El solar en el que se halla situada su casa, ejemplo de este vínculo, es un emplazamiento en el que también se abrieron canteras para extraer roca y piedra, y la masa forestal se ha ido sacrificando para cortar madera destinada a servir de leña y otros usos. Kamath House trata de cicatrizar las heridas de la tierra y establecer una pequeña zona en el ecosistema que regenere verde y cree espacio y estética mediante un cambio de los materiales usados en y alrededor del solar. Una arquitectura que realce, cuide y mime el carácter de los elementos de la naturaleza. Kamath House es un espacio representativo de un estilo de vida en donde el modelo humano dentro de la naturaleza está en continua evolución.

Architects: **Revathi & Vasant Kamath**

Location: **Hauz Khas, South Delhi – India**

Nalin Tomar's Tower House

Photographer: **Satoshi Asakawa**   Completion date: **1992**

The irregular, L-shape, 430 sq. ft. plot of the Tower House overlooks the spectacular Hauz Khas monuments. The longer part of the L, with a front wall some 30 feet long overlooking the monuments, is organized on five different levels. The basement contains the dining-room, pantry and kitchen; the ground floor houses the study; the mezzanine, the guest bedroom; the first floor, the living room, and the second floor, the master bedroom and terrace. The shorter section, 7 feet wide, provides the access to the house at the end of an alleyway. This part contains the staircase, with the landings extended to house the entrance lobby, a fountain, the toilets and a water tank.

Das unregelmäßige, L-förmige, 40 m² große Grundstück des Tower House schaut auf die spektakulären Denkmäler von Hauz Khas. Der längere Arm des L, der mit einer Vorderfront von 8 m auf die Denkmäler blickt, ist in fünf Ebenen unterteilt. Im Untergeschoss befinden sich Küche, Vorratskammer und Esszimmer, im Erdgeschoss das Arbeitszimmer, im Zwischengeschoss das Gästezimmer, im ersten Stock das Wohnzimmer und im zweiten Stock das Schlafzimmer des Eigentümers und die Terrasse. Der kürzere, 2 m breite Arm gewährleistet den Zugang zu diesem am Ende einer Gasse gelegenem Haus. Hier liegt die Treppe, auf deren vergrößerten Absätzen sich der Eingangsflur, ein Springbrunnen, eine Toilette und ein Wassertank befinden.

Le terrain irrégulier en L, de 40 m², de la Tower House surplombe les spectaculaires monuments Hauz Khas. La longueur du L, avec une façade de 8 m donnant sur les monuments, est organisée sur cinq niveaux. Le sous-sol accueille les repas, la réserve et la cuisine, le rez-de-chaussée l'atelier, la mezzanine la chambre d'hôte, le premier le séjour et le second la chambre principale et la terrasse. D'accès étroit, 2 m de large, la largeur du terrain intègre la maison au bout d'un chemin. Elle abrite l'escalier dont les paliers s'élargissent pour le couloir d'entrée, la fontaine, les toilettes et un réservoir d'eau.

El irregular terreno en forma de L de 40 m² en donde se ubica la Tower House domina la espectacular vista de los monumentos de Hauz Khas. La parte más larga de esta L, constituida por un muro frontal de unos 8 m que da a los monumentos, está ordenada en cinco niveles. El sótano da cabida al comedor, a la bodega y a la cocina; la planta baja, al estudio; el entresuelo alberga la habitación de invitados; el primer piso, el salón, y en la segunda planta se encuentran la habitación principal y la terraza. Su parte más estrecha, de 2 m de anchura, facilita el acceso a la casa situada al extremo de un callejón del barrio. Esta parte contiene las escaleras, cuyo rellano se ha ampliado para albergar el vestíbulo de la entrada, una fuente, los lavabos y también un depósito de agua.

Site plan

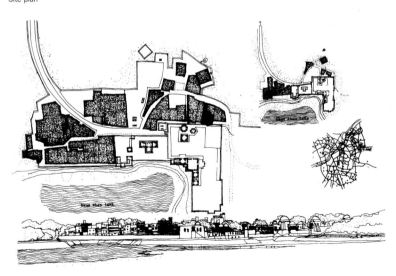

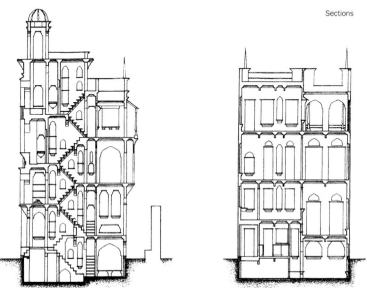

Sections

Architects: **Budiman Hendropurnomo – Denton Corker Marshall**

Location: **Bali – Indonesia**

Maya Ubud Balinese Villa

Photographer: **Denton Corker Marshall** Completion date: **2002**

This Balinese villa forms part of the Maya Ubud resort complex, situated on a long peninsular that gradually slopes down to the southern part of the island before dropping off dramatically at the southernmost tip, where a spa is situated, on the banks of the river Petanu. The whole area between the rivers Petanu and Pakerisan not only abounds in remains of prehistoric Bali but is also considered sacred. Maya Ubud juggles with the new and the traditional in every part of its design. Its architecture is sustainable, with bamboo, thatched alang-alang roofs, and soft river stone as their main components. Bali's culture and heritage are celebrated in every nook and cranny.

Diese balinesische Villa gehört zu der Maya Ubud Wohnsiedlung, die auf einer sich bis nach Südbali erstreckenden länglichen Halbinsel liegt, die kontinuierlich und schließlich an ihrem südlichsten Ende steil abfällt, dort nämlich, wo sich ein Kurort am Ufer des Flusses Petanu befindet. Das gesamte zwischen den beiden Flüssen Petanu und Pakerisan liegende Gebiet weist zahlreiche antike Funde aus dem prähistorischen Bali auf und ist den Balinesen heilig. Das Design von Maya Ubud jongliert mit traditionellen und modernen Konzepten. Die Architektur beruft sich auf traditionelle Materialien, wie vor allem Bambus, Strohdächer im alang-alang-Stil und weicher Flussstein. Balinesische Kultur und Tradition zeigen sich hier in jedem Winkel.

Cette villa balinaise intègre le complexe de villégiature Maya Ubud, situé sur une longue péninsule descendant graduellement vers le sud de Bali, avant de chuter spectaculairement à l'extrémité méridionale où une station thermale s'invite au bord de la rivière Petanu. La zone délimitée par les deux rivières, Petanu et Pakerisan, riche en antiquités balinaises préhistoriques, est aussi nommée la terre sainte. Maya Ubud jongle avec les concepts, comme l'ancien et le nouveau, dans tout son design. L'architecture est viable, bambou, toit chaumé d'alang-alang et pierres lisses de rivières étant les composants essentiels. La culture et l'héritage balinais sont célébrés en tout point.

Este chalé balinés forma parte del conjunto residencial denominado Maya Ubud, situado en un terreno que adopta las formas de una larga península que desciende de manera gradual hacia la parte sur de la isla antes de caer de forma pronunciada en su extremo sur, lugar en el cual se halla ubicado un balneario, a orillas del río Petanu. A esta zona, rica en restos antiguos del Bali prehistórico, y que delimita con los dos ríos Petanu y Pakerisan, se la conoce también como tierra sagrada. El diseño de Maya Ubud juega constantemente con los conceptos de lo nuevo y lo tradicional. Con una arquitectura sostenible, utilizando el bambú, piedra suave de río y techos de paja tipo "alang-alang" como elementos principales, el patrimonio cultural de la isla se hace patente por doquier.

Architect: **Irianto Purnomo Hadi**

Location: **Jakarta – Indonesia**

Pondok Indah House

Photographer: **Satoshi Asakawa**   Completion date: 2000

Irianto Purnomo Hadi, a founding member of AMI (Arsitek Muda Indonesia), designed this two-and-half story house, featuring six split-floor levels and located in the residential Pondok Indah district in South Jakarta, on a corner plot measuring some 6,500 sq. ft. Its owners, a couple with a daughter, asked the architect to make the most of the sweeping view of Jakarta to the east, which stretches for almost 180 degrees. The living room and the upper-level sitting room were thus both positioned facing east, with an array of windows and large pivoted glass doors. The main staircase, placed right in the center of the house, climbs up behind the lounge areas, and all the other rooms are organized around it.

Irianto Purnomo Hadi, ein Gründermitglied von AMI (Arsitek Muda Indonesia), entwarf dieses zweieinhalbstöckige Haus mit sechs verschiedenen Ebenen, das in dem Wohngebiet Pondok Indah in Süd-Jakarta auf einem 600 m² großen Eckgrundstück entstand. Die Eigentümer, Ehepaar und Tochter, baten den Architekten, das Beste aus dem sich im Winkel von beinahe 180 Grad nach Osten ausbreitende Panorama auf die Stadt Jakarta zu machen. Das Wohnzimmer und der auf der oberen Ebene gelegene Salon wurden aus diesem Grund nach Osten gerichtet, mit einer Reihe Fenster und drehbaren Glastüren. Im Zentrum des Hauses liegt die Haupttreppe des Gebäudes, die hinter den Wohnräumen emporführt und um die sich alle weiteren Räume organisieren.

Irianto Purnomo Hadi, membre fondateur d'AMI (Arsitek Muda Indonesia), a pensé cette maison de deux niveaux et demi, présentant six demi-niveaux et située dans le quartier résidentiel de Pondok Indah au sud de Djakarta, sur un site carré de 600 m². Ses propriétaires, un couple et leur fille, souhaitaient maximiser la superbe vue à l'Est, un panorama de près de 180 degrés sur Djakarta. Le séjour et le salon du niveau supérieur ont été exposés à l'Est, en multipliant les ouvertures, grâce à grandes portes vitrées pivotantes. Au-delà de ces pièces, l'escalier principal de la demeure est situé pratiquement au cœur même de la maison. Toutes les autres pièces gravitent autour de lui.

Irianto Purnomo Hadi, miembro fundador de Arsitek Muda Indonesia (AMI), diseñó esta vivienda de dos pisos y medio, con seis niveles de suelo diferenciado, la cual se halla ubicada en un solar de unos 600 m² situado en una zona residencial del sur de Yakarta denominada Pondok Indah. Sus propietarios, un matrimonio con una hija, requirieron al arquitecto que sacara el máximo partido de la amplia vista de casi 180 grados que podía divisarse, al este, de la ciudad de Yakarta. Para ello, el arquitecto situó el comedor y una sala de estar hacia esta dirección, y recurrió a muchos ventanales y a grandes puertas de cristal giratorias. Detrás del comedor y la sala de estar se halla la principal escalera de la vivienda, ubicada justo en el centro de la casa y alrededor de la cual se sitúan el resto de sus estancias.

Architect: **Adi Purnomo**

Location: **Jakarta – Indonesia**

Cutting Wall

Photographer: **Satoshi Asakawa** Completion date: 1998

Adi Purnomo makes it clear that although "Cutting Wall" looks like a three-story building, it is in fact a two-story house. The height of the building results from the insertion of what the architect calls a "generator of natural air circulation", a large opening in the rooftop that serves to direct fresh air into the interior of the building. The owner wanted to renovate this house, set in a lower-middle class residential area on the outskirts of Jakarta, in order to gain more space and cool down the temperature inside. For the latter, the architect drew on Indonesia's traditional roofing design, specifically designed to provide a house with natural ventilation. This meant that he had to rule out the use of a sloping roof .

Obwohl „Cutting Wall" einem dreistöckigen Gebäude gleicht, handelt es sich laut Adi Purnomo um ein zweistöckiges Wohnhaus. Die Höhe des Hauses beruht auf dem sogenannten „natural air circulation generator", einer ins Dach eingelassenen Spalte, durch die Frischluft bis ins Erdgeschoss zirkuliert. Der Eigentümer wünschte mit der Renovierung dieses Hauses, welches sich in einem Wohngebiet der unteren Mittelschicht von Jakarta befindet, mehr Raum und eine kühlere Raumtemperatur zu erreichen. Diese Aufgaben wurden erfüllt, indem der Architekt statt des typischen Giebeldaches das traditionelle indonesische Dach wählte, welches seit jeher eine bessere Ventilation gewährleistete.

A di Purnomo l'annonce clairement : « Cutting Wall » ressemble à une maison de trois étages mais c'est une demeure à deux niveaux. L'édifice est grand de par l'introduction de ce que l'architecte appelle « générateur de circulation d'air naturel », une fente du toit propulsant l'air frais vers le bas de la maison. Dans une zone résidentielle moyenne de la banlieue de Djakarta, le propriétaire voulait rénover le lieu pour gagner de l'espace tout rafraîchissant l'intérieur. L'architecte contrôle la température en rejetant le toit en pente, typique, pour révéler la fonction du toit indonésien traditionnel, dont la ventilation naturelle fut toujours un point essentiel.

A di Purnomo afirma que aunque "Cutting Wall" parezca una casa de tres pisos es en realidad una vivienda de dos. La altura del edificio se debe a que el arquitecto introdujo lo que el denomina un "generador para hacer circular aire natural", que consiste en una amplia abertura en el tejado que lleva aire fresco hacia el interior del edificio. Ubicado en una zona residencial de clase media-baja de las afueras de Yakarta, su propietario quería remodelar su vivienda para ganar más espacio y refrigerar la temperatura de su interior. Para conseguirlo, el arquitecto recurrió a la tradicional cubierta indonesia, específicamente diseñada para proveer a la casa de ventilación natural de la casa. Para ello sacrifica el techo en pendiente.

Architects: **Ang Gin Wah – Gin + design workshop**

Location: **Singapore**

Ee House

Photographer: **Satoshi Asakawa**   Completion date: **1996**

Ang Gin Wah describes Ee House as a project that addresses and confronts the situation of the modern urban environment. It also tackles the history of its setting and the strict building regulations in force in the area. Such flexibility and complexity requires the design to deal with each micro-function separately; so, the architect came up with three basic "houses" or units connected by a common veranda. Each "house" is basically defined by the use allotted to it and, although all of them function as independent units, there is an ever-present dialogue with the other parts of the home, thanks to the clear physical connection between them.

Laut Ang Gin Wah richtet sich Ee House an das existierende urbane Gefüge und antwortet ebenso auf die Geschichte seines Ortes wie die strengen städtischen Bauvorschriften dieses Gebietes. Solche Flexibilität und Komplexität verlangt einen Entwurf, der die Mikrofunktionen eines Hauses einzeln behandelt und den Architekten dazu veranlasste, drei durch eine gemeinsame Galerie miteinander verbundene „Häuser" bzw. Wohneinheiten zu entwickeln. Jedes dieser drei „Häuser" definiert sich eindeutig aus seinem allgemeinen Gebrauch heraus und kann auch unabhängig von den anderen funktionieren, während der Dialog untereinander durch eine eindeutige, physische Verbindung erhalten bleibt.

Selon Ang Gin Wah, Ee House répond à un tissu urbain existant, mais aussi à l'histoire du lieu et aux normes strictes de construction de la zone. Cette flexibilité et cette complexité exigent que le design traite les micro-fonctions séparément, d'où le développement de trois « maisons » ou unités basiques enfichées dans une galerie commune. Chacune, clairement définie par son usage général, peut fonctionner isolément tout en dialoguant avec les autres via un lien visible et physique.

Ang Gin Wah describe la Ee House como un proyecto que trata y afronta la cuestión de la situación del tejido urbano actual. Trata también de la historia del lugar donde se halla ubicada, y además confronta las estrictas normas de construcción vigentes en la zona. Tal flexibilidad y complejidad requieren que su diseño trate por separado cada una de las microfunciones que se puedan dar en la vivienda. Así pues, el arquitecto desarrolló tres casas o unidades básicas que conectan a una galería común. Cada una de ellas viene definida en general por el uso que se le asigna. Aun así, puede funcionar como unidad independiente, aunque manteniendo siempre un diálogo con las otras unidades o casas, mediante una obvia conexión física.

Architects: **Bedmar & Shi Design Consultants**

Location: **Singapore**

The Friedland House

Photographer: **Ernesto Bedmar**   Completion date: **2000**

The organization of this house is similar to that of many Bedmar & Shi designs; that is, a U-shape courtyard unified by a pool and a lawn. The composition of the house is divided into three sections. The first, containing the main entrance, spans two stories, while a single-story block holds the main living room. The two-floor section lying parallel to the living-room block contains the kitchen, dining room and guest room on the ground floor, with the master bedroom on the first floor. According to Mr. Bedmar, the simplicity of the layout and the understatement of the entrance belie the sense of "promontory" drama evoked by the house. The entire structure of the house built in solid teak and, overall, its architecture is highly sensitive to the traditions of South-East Asia.

Dieses Haus ist ähnlich wie die anderen von Bedmar & Shi entworfenen Häuser angelegt, nämlich um einen Hof in U-Form, den Schwimmbad und Rasenfläche vereinheitlichen. Es ist in drei Abschnitte aufgeteilt: der erste, zweistöckige, beherbergt den Haupteingang, während in einem anderen, einstöckigen, das Wohnzimmer liegt. Parallel zu diesem verläuft ein dritter zweistöckiger Flügel, in dem im ersten Stock Küche, Ess- und Gästezimmer und im zweiten Stock das Schlafzimmer des Besitzers untergebracht sind. Die Schlichtheit dieses Projekts und das Understatement seiner Eingangshalle täuschen uns, laut Bedmar, über das dramatische Erleben des „Vorgebirges" hinweg, welches dieses Haus uns suggeriert. Die ganze Struktur des Hauses ist aus Teakholz angefertigt, und seine gesamte Architektur eine Anlehnung an die Empfindsamkeit südostasiatischer Traditionen.

Cette maison s'organise comme beaucoup de réalisations de Bedmar & Shi designs : une cour formée par un plan en U, unifié par la piscine et la pelouse. La composition des lieux repose sur trois blocs. Le premier, formant l'entrée principale, est haut de deux niveaux alors qu'un bloc d'un seul étage accueille le séjour. Le bloc double parallèle au bloc de séjour comprend cuisine, salle à manger et chambre d'hôte au rez-de-chaussée et la suite principale au premier. La simplicité de la stratégie de disposition et la discrétion de l'entrée contredisent, selon M. Bedmar, le sens du dramatique « promontoire » offert par les lieux. La structure complète, en teck massif, et l'architecture de la demeure assimilent les sensibilités des traditions du Sud-Est asiatique.

Este edificio ha sido concebido con un estilo similar a otros proyectos firmados por Bedmar & Shi, es decir, un diseño formado por un patio en forma de U unido por la piscina y el césped. La organización de la casa define tres secciones o bloques. El primero, de dos pisos de altura, alberga la entrada principal. Otro bloque de un piso contiene el salón principal. En el volumen de dos pisos paralelo al del salón se encuentran la cocina, el comedor y una habitación para huéspedes en la planta baja y la habitación principal en el primer piso. La sencillez del proyecto y el comedido diseño de su entrada no dejan traslucir, según Bedmar, la sensación de "drama promontorio" que esta vivienda sugiere. La estructura total de la casa, construida en madera de teca, y su arquitectura en general asumen y recogen las sensibilidades de las tradiciones del sudeste asiático.

Architects: **Frank Ling & Pilar González-Herraiz –**

architron design consultants

Location: **Selangor – Malaysia**

Dialogue House

hotographers: **Satoshi Asakawa & Frank Ling** Completion date: **1998**

The company architron built this spacious house for Mr. and Mrs. Koay. It is located on the MultimediaSuperCorridor (MSC) in Kuala Lumpur, an up-market holiday resort organized around a golf course. The house is characterized by the large creases on its aluminum roof, which covers a number of forms set in a flexible configuration of two rows, each containing various rooms. A large, two-story high atrium separates the two rows and forms the nucleus of the house. The east row is a more private area with bedrooms, bathrooms and a study, while the west row provides guest rooms, kitchens and a large living room. González and Ling embedded the house into the landscape by creating a structure that gives its occupants stunning views of the exterior.

Dieses Haus wurde von der Firma architron für das Ehepaar Koay gebaut und befindet sich im MultimediaSuperCorridor (MSC) von Kuala Lumpur, einer exklusiven Ferienanlage, in deren Mitte ein Golfplatz angelegt ist. Das große gefaltete Aluminiumdach, unter dem sich in zwei Blöcken lose angeordnet verschieden geformte, mehrere Räume umfassende Baukörper befinden, ist das Hauptmerkmal dieses Hauses. Ein großes sich über zwei Stockwerke erstreckendes Atrium trennt die beiden Blöcke voneinander und bildet das Herzstück des Hauses. Während im privateren Ostflügel Schlafzimmer, Bäder und ein Arbeitszimmer liegen, befinden sich im Westflügel Gästezimmer, Küche und ein großes Wohnzimmer. González und Ling haben das Haus, das den Bewohnern wunderbare Panoramen auf die umliegende Landschaft bietet, in seine Umgebung eingebettet.

L'entreprise architron a construit cette vaste maison isolée pour le couple Koay. La rési-dence se situe sur le MultimediaSuperCorridor (MSC) de Kuala Lumpur, une station de luxe dotée d'un parcours de golf. La maison se caractérise par les grands plans plissés du toit d'aluminium, couvrant plusieurs volumes disposés librement sur deux rangs. Ces volu-mes abritent les pièces. Un grand atrium, de deux niveaux, sépare les deux rangs et forme le cœur de la maison. Le rang est contient une aire privée avec chambres, bains et un bureau. Le rang ouest héberge les invités, des cuisines et le grand séjour. González et Ling ont serti la maison dans le paysage en faisant dialoguer intérieur et extérieur grâce à des vues et des aperçus à travers la structure.

La firma architron levantó esta espaciosa casa para el matrimonio Koay, ubicada en el conocido MultimediaSuperCorridor (MSC) de Kuala Lumpur, un exclusivo centro vaca-cional en medio del cual se encuentra un campo de golf. El edificio se caracteriza por los grandes pliegues de la cubierta de aluminio, bajo la que descansan varios volúmenes dis-puestos en dos hileras. Un gran atrio de dos pisos de altura separa las dos hileras forman-do el núcleo del conjunto. En la hilera de la parte derecha se encuentran las estancias pri-vadas, con las habitaciones de sus propietarios, los baños y un estudio. En la de la parte izquierda se ubican las habitaciones para invitados, las cocinas y un gran salón. González y Ling logran integrar la casa en el paisaje circundante mediante una estructura que ofrece a sus residentes espléndidas vistas panorámicas.

Architects: **Frank Ling & Pilar González-Herraiz –**
architron design consultants
Location: **Kuala Lumpur – Malaysia**

Casa Bosco

Photographer: **Satoshi Asakawa** Completion date: **2000**

Frank Ling, from Malaysia, and Pilar González-Herraiz, from Spain, met while they were both studying architecture at the famous AA School in London. After getting married, they set up their own architectural studio, architron, and designed their own private apartment, known as Casa Bosco, where they now live. The interior comprises two 1300 sq. ft. apartments inside a four-story block built in the 1960s. Each unit originally had two bedrooms, one bathroom, a lounge-dining room, a kitchen and a small service area. When González and Ling designed their home, they sought to maintain and even intensify the feeling of open space evident in the existing design by creating new perspectives, but without losing the spirit of the original. architron used color as the main element for bringing greater definition to the various spaces.

Der Malaysier Frank Ling lernte die Spanierin Pilar González-Herraiz während ihres gemeinsamen Architekturstudiums an der berühmten AA School in London kennen. Das Architektenehepaar gründete das Büro architron und entwarf Casa Bosco, ihre Privatwohnung. Es besteht aus zwei je 120 m² großen Apartments in einem vierstöckigen Gebäude aus den 1960er Jahren, wovon jedes ursprünglich zwei Schlafzimmer, ein Bad, ein Wohn- und Esszimmer, eine Küche und kleine Kammer besaß. Die schon im alten Entwurf angestrebte räumliche Großzügigkeit sollte bewahrt und erweitert werden, indem eine neue Perspektive geschaffen wurde, ohne den Geist der alten gänzlich zu verlieren. architrons Gebrauch von Farben als wesentliche Elemente verleiht den jeweiligen Räumen Ausdruck.

Frank Ling, natif de Malaisie, et Pilar González-Herraiz, d'Espagne, se sont connus en étudiant l'architecture à la célèbre AA School, à Londres. Ce couple marié a monté son propre cabinet, architron, et conçu son propre appartement, où ils résident, pour le baptiser Casa Bosco. L'intérieur est une composition de deux appartements de 120 m² dans un bloc de quatre étages des années 1960. Chaque unité offrait deux chambres, un bain, une pièce repas/séjour, une cuisine et une petite pièce de service. Les architectes souhaitaient retenir et diffuser l'évidente sensation d'ouverture du concept d'origine, le sens de l'espace dans l'espace, créant une autre perspective mais en préservant la mémoire originelle. La couleur sert à définir davantage les espaces.

Frank Ling, de Malasia, y Pilar González-Herraiz, de España, se conocieron estudiando Arquitectura en la prestigiosa AA School de Londres. El matrimonio estableció el taller de arquitectura, architron, y diseñó el apartamento en el que residen actualmente, conocido como Casa Bosco. El interior está formado por dos pisos de 120 m² cada uno situados en un edifcio de cuatro plantas de los años sesenta. Cada uno albergaba inicialmente dos habitaciones, un baño, salón comedor, cocina y una pequeña área de servicio. Los arquitectos quisieron conservar y aumentar la sensación de espacios abiertos ya existente, con una nueva perspectiva pero manteniendo el espíritu del original. Para una mayor definición de los diversos espacios, architron recurre al uso del color como elemento principal.

Architects: **Kanika R'kul – Leigh & Orange (Thailand) Ltd.**

Location: **Bangkok – Thailand**

House U3

Photographers: **Skyline Studio, Kanika R'kul** Completion date: **1997**

House U3 consists of a main building, a kitchen unit and a garage, which together form a U-shape courtyard. It was built to be shared by the architect herself with her parents, her sister and a maid. The underlying tension of House U3 lies in Kanika R'kul's attempt to explore the relationship between the permeation of Western culture and values, further emphasized by the architect's own education in the West, and the move from the traditional to the modern in the Thai lifestyle, reflected in the architect's attempt to come to terms with her origins through architecture. House U3 endeavours to define a position where the two sets of values co-exist, without necessarily taking sides.

House U3 bildet mit einem Haupthaus, einem Küchengebäude und einer Garage einen U-förmigen Hof und wird von der Architektin selbst, ihren Eltern, ihrer Schwester und einem Hausmädchen bewohnt. Die dem Haus zugrunde liegende Spannung besteht in der Auseinandersetzung der Einfluss nehmenden westlichen Kultur und Wertvorstellungen einerseits, verstärkt durch das Studium der Architektin in der Westlichen Welt, mit der Entwicklung vom traditionellen zum modernen thailändischen Lebensstil, widergespiegelt im Versuch der Architektin durch ihre Arbeit zu ihren Wurzeln zu finden. Mit dem Haus soll eine Position definiert werden, in der beide Wertvorstellungen nebeneinander existieren, ohne dass einer der Vorrang gegeben wird.

House U3 comprend l'édifice principal, la cuisine et le garage, définissant une cour en U. L'architecte l'a créé pour ses parents, sa sœur, une femme de chambre et lui-même. Le défi sous-jacent de House U3 se trouve dans la tentative de l'architecte d'explorer la relation entre l'influence culturelle et les valeurs occidentales, soulignées par sa propre formation en occident, et le passage d'un mode de vie traditionnel thaïlandais à la modernité, accentué par la tentative de l'architecte d'être en phase avec ses origines par son art. La maison veut définir une position où deux valeurs coexistent mais sans prendre partie.

House U3 está formada por un edificio principal, un módulo con cocina y un garaje, que perfilan el conjunto un patio que tiene forma de U. Se construyó para albergar a los padres de la arquitecta, su hermana, una sirvienta y también para ella misma. En House U3 se observa la lucha subyacente de la arquitecta por intentar explorar la relación entre la penetración e impregnación de la cultura y valores occidentales, en parte puesta de relieve por su propia formación en Occidente, y la transformación de lo tradicional en lo moderno en las pautas de vida en Tailandia, también resaltada por los esfuerzos de la arquitecta en ponerse de acuerdo con sus orígenes mediante la arquitectura. House U3 intenta definir una posición intermedia en la que ambos valores coexisten sin tomar partido por ninguno en particular.

Architect: **Antonio Eraso**

Location: **Bangkok – Thailand**

Tsao + Robinson Apartment

Photographer: **Antonio Eraso** Completion date: **2000**

The owners of this apartment—an American couple living in South-East Asia, with Bangkok as their base—wanted to free their 3-bedroom penthouse from its original segmented configuration into a more efficient and uncluttered single space, while still retaining private spaces, such as bedrooms. The interior walls were removed almost entirely to provide greater openness and clarity. The primary aim was to create a succession of spaces that interweaved with one another to allowing the couple, and their only daughter, to enjoy a free space. In order to be able to receive their frequent visitors, one of the bedrooms was transformed into a multiple-purpose room that can be quickly and easily turned into a more private space for the benefit of guests.

Die Eigentümer dieses Apartments, ein amerikanisches, in Südostasien lebendes Ehepaar, die Bangkok zu ihrer Heimat gemacht haben, wollten mit dem Umbau dieses Penthauses mit 3 Schlafzimmern das ursprüngliche, unterteilte Raumprogramm in eine funktionellere offenere Wohnfläche umwandeln, ohne die Intimität der Schlafzimmer aufzugeben. Um die gewünschte Weiträumigkeit und Transparenz zu erzielen, wurden fast alle Innenwände beseitigt. Das Ziel war es, eine Reihe aufeinanderfolgender und in sich verwobener Räume zu leben, die dem Ehepaar und ihrer Tochter erlauben, in einem einzigen Raum zu leben. Um die häufigen Gäste zu beherbergen, wurde einer des Schlafzimmer zu einem Allzweckraum, der sich problemlos und schnell in ein Gästezimmer verwandeln lässt.

Les propriétaires, un couple américain vivant dans le Sud-Est asiatique avec Bangkok comme base principale, voulaient modifier la disposition segmentée et fractionnée d'un penthouse de 3 chambres en un « espace unique », plus efficace et dépouillé, tout en préservant les espaces intimes, ainsi les chambres. La plupart des murs intérieurs a été retirée afin d'ouvrir et de clarifier le plan. Dès le début, l'objectif était la création d'une série d'espaces successifs s'entrelaçant entre eux et permettant au couple, et à leur fille unique, de jouir d'un espace d'un seul tenant. Pour accueillir leurs visiteurs fréquents, une des chambres est devenue une pièce à usages multiples, aisément et rapidement convertible d'un espace ouvert en un chambre d'hôte.

Los propietarios, una pareja estadounidense residente en el sudeste asiático con Bangkok como principal plataforma para viajar por la zona, querían transformar la configuración segmentada y fraccionada inicial de este ático en un espacio único, aun cuando optaran por mantener áreas privadas como las habitaciones. Se eliminaron casi todas las paredes interiores para disponer de más claridad y transparencia. Desde un principio se fijaron como meta crear un conjunto de áreas que al entretejerse una con otra daban a sus propietarios y a su única hija la posibilidad de disfrutar de un solo espacio. Con el fin de poder recibir a sus frecuentes visitantes, una de las habitaciones se transformó en un espacio multiuso que permitía una rápida y fácil conversión en un espacio más privado.

Floor plan

Architects: **Naonori Matsuda + Zhu Xiao Yun**

Location: **Hong Kong – China**

Atelier ZAM

Photographer: **Satoshi Asakawa** Completion date: **2000**

Naonori Matsuda is a Japanese architect who has been living for over 20 years in Hong Kong, where he teaches architectural theory in the university. The renovation of this 40-year old apartment involved the removal of all the non-structural walls thus converting the original three bedrooms with its two bathrooms into one large space that serves both as an office and as a home for the architect's family. Two large sliding doors provide temporary privacy for a bedroom at nighttime, while at other times it functions as a living room, guestroom or playroom for the architect's young daughter. The ceiling closets run all along the main beams, providing abundant storage space.

Naonori Matsuda ist ein japanischer Architekt, der seit über 20 Jahren in Hongkong lebt, wo er an der Universität Architekturtheorie lehrt. Bei der Renovierung dieser 40 Jahre alten Wohnung wurden alle Trennwände beseitigt und aus den ehemaligen drei Schlafzimmern und zwei Bädern entstand eine einzige großzügige Fläche, die der Architektenfamilie sowohl als Büro als auch als Wohnung dient. Zwei große Schiebetüren garantieren des Nachts Intimität im Schlafzimmer, während dieses am Tage auch als Wohnraum, Gästezimmer oder Spielzimmer für die kleine Tochter fungiert. Die unterhalb der Decke eingefügten Wandschränke ziehen sich an den Hauptbalken entlang und schaffen reichlich Stauraum.

Naonori Matsuda est un architecte japonais résident à Hong Kong depuis plus de 20 ans, enseignant l'architecture théorique à l'Université de Hong Kong. La rénovation de cet appartement de 40 ans a vu le retrait de tous les murs non structuraux, convertissant ainsi les trois chambres et deux bains d'origine en un vaste espace unique, à la fois bureau et demeure pour l'architecte et sa famille. Deux grands panneaux coulissants offrent à la chambre une intimité nocturne provisoire devenant, de jour, un salon, chambre d'invité ou salle de jeux pour leur jeune fille. Les placards au plafond parcourent les poutres, offrant un espace de rangement abondant.

Naonori Matsuda es un arquitecto japonés residente en Hong Kong desde hace más de 20 años, en cuya universidad enseña teoría de la arquitectura. Para la reforma de este apartamento de 40 años de antigüedad se eliminaron todos los tabiques, transformando el área original de tres habitaciones y dos baños en un amplio y único espacio utilizado tanto para oficina como para vivienda del arquitecto y su familia. Dos grandes puertas correderas dan a la estancia la privacidad nocturna necesaria, mientras que de día adopta la función de salón, habitación de invitados o cuarto de juegos para la hija. Los armarios, a lo largo de las vigas principales del techo, proporcionan abundante espacio para guardar cosas.

Architect: **e'vision (architects & associates) ltd.**

Location: **Hong Kong – China**

Standford Villa

Photographer: **e'vision** Completion date: **1999**

The owner of this apartment works in finance, and the demanding pace of his occupation led him to look for a haven of tranquility where he could wind down when he came back from work. The careful organization of all the elements in this project allowed the designers to create a minimalist, functional apartment that exudes an all-embracing Zen-like calm. The attention to detail is meticulous, with all sockets and wiring kept out of sight to allow the purity of the design to remain intact. Although the apartment is small, its sense of space enables the visitor to understand and appreciate the efficient positioning of essential objects.

Der Eigentümer dieser Wohnung ist im Finanzwesen tätig, und aufgrund seiner enormen Arbeitsanforderungen wünschte er eine Oase der Ruhe, um nach der Arbeit abschalten zu können. Die behutsame Organisation aller Elemente in diesem Projekt erlaubten den Designern, ein minimalistisches und funktionales Apartment zu erschaffen, dem eine Zen-gleiche Gelassenheit innewohnt. Den Details wurde große Aufmerksamkeit geschenkt und alle Steckdosen und Leitungen so verlegt, dass die Reinheit des Designs ungestört blieb. Obwohl sehr klein, vermittelt das Apartment ein Raumgefühl, welches dem Besucher ermöglicht, die wirksame Platzierung einzelner Objekte zu verstehen und zu würdigen.

Le propriétaire des lieux est un financier et, en raison du rythme exigeant de sa profession, requiert que son foyer soit un havre de paix pour s'échapper après le travail. L'organisation précise de chaque élément du projet permet aux designers de créer un lieu minimaliste et fonctionnel, diffusant une atmosphère générale de calme zen. L'attention au détail est absolue, prises et câbles étant escamotés afin de préserver la pureté du design. L'appartement, bien que petit, offre un sens de l'espace permettant au visiteur de comprendre et d'apprécier la disposition efficiente des objets essentiels.

El propietario de este apartamento es un profesional de las finanzas. Debido al ritmo de su trabajo, quería que su apartamento fuera un mar de tranquilidad en donde refugiarse después del trabajo diario. La esmerada organización de todos los elementos de este proyecto permitió diseñar un apartamento minimalista y funcional que ofrece un ambiente de total calma al estilo zen. La atención dada a los detalles es absoluta, ocultando enchufes e instalación eléctrica en general para mantener así intacta la pureza del diseño. Aunque el apartamento sea de reducidas dimensiones, su sensación de espacio permite al visitante apreciar y comprender la manera eficiente cómo están colocados los objetos indispensables.

Architect: **e'vision (architects & associates) ltd.**

Location: **Hong Kong – China**

King's Park Villa

Photographer: **e'vision** Completion date: **2000**

This apartment, originally just another of Hong Kong's countless box-like homes, was converted into a fairy-tale setting that blends mystery, nature and dream in a futuristic approach. In keeping with the client's main design brief—that the space reflected his own personality—the architects made use of fiberglass columns to divide the main room into dining and living areas, both equipped with computerized light sensors. Depending on the owner's mood when he enters his home, he can pre-set different environments through combinations of lighting, music, etc., creating a very special atmosphere.

Dieses Apartment, ursprünglich eines der vielen schachtelähnlichen Wohnungen von Hongkong, wurde in eine märchenhafte Szenerie verwandelt, in dem sich Mystik, Natur und Traum in einer futuristischen Annäherung zusammenfügen. Um dem Wunsch des Auftragsgebers gerecht zu werden, der in der Wohnung seine eigene Persönlichkeit reflektiert sehen möchte, benutzten die Architekten zur Unterteilung der Wohnfläche Pfeiler aus Fiberglas, und statteten das so entstandene Wohn- und Esszimmer mit computergesteuerten Lichtsensoren aus. Der Eigentümer kann so je nach Laune verschiedene Stimmungen durch unterschiedliche Beleuchtung, Musik etc., vorprogrammieren und eine ganz besondere Atmosphäre schaffen.

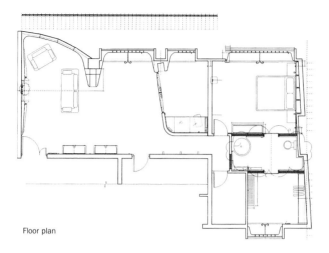

Floor plan

Cet appartement, à l'origine si typique des logements diminutifs de Hong Kong, a converti son espace en une scène de conte de fées mêlant mystère, nature et approche futuriste onirique. Respectant l'essence de la commande du client, le lieu reflétant sa personnalité, les architectes ont employé des colonnes de fibre de verre pour diviser la pièce principale pour les repas et le séjour, les équipant de capteurs de lumières à processeur. Selon l'humeur du résident en entrant dans l'appartement, il est possible de prédéfinir diverses ambiances par l'éclairage, la musique, etc., créant une atmosphère très spéciale.

Este apartamento, originalmente una de tantas diminutas viviendas típicas de Hong Kong, ha visto transformado su espacio en un escenario de ensueño que funde juntos misterio, carácter y fantasía en una propuesta futurista. Dando respuesta a las instrucciones básicas de su cliente para que el lugar reflejara las características de su personalidad, los arquitectos utilizaron columnas de fibra de vidrio para dividir la estancia principal en dos áreas, comedor y salón, ambas equipadas con sensores de luz computerizados. En función del estado de ánimo que tenga el propietario al acceder a su casa, éste puede programar con anterioridad diversos ambientes mediante los juegos de luces, de la música... para crear una atmósfera muy particular.

Architect: **Gary Chang – Edge Design Institute Ltd.**

Location: **Hong Kong – China**

Gary's Apartment

Photographer: **Almond Chu** Completion date: 1999

The confined space in this apartment, some 330 sq. ft., is home to a famous young Hong Kong architect. The flexibility and multiple uses of the partitions, lighting, and mobile furniture have resulted in a space that is open and totally versatile. The main opening—the window overlooking the street—offers various different views of the world outside—whether the actual view out of the window or, on the large-scale screen, the fantasy world of Hollywood or the virtual reality of the Internet. The pervading atmosphere remind movie fans of some of the fascinating scenes in the work of Wong Kar-Wai.

Dieses nur 30 m² große Apartment wird von einem berühmten jungen Architekten aus Hongkong bewohnt. Dank der unterschiedlichen und vielfältigen Verwendung von Trennwänden, Beleuchtung und leicht verstellbarem Mobiliar entsteht ein offener und vollkommen wandelbarer Raum. Die vordere Fensterfront bietet verschiedenste Panoramen, sei es der aktuelle Blick aus dem Fenster, sei es die auf den großen Bildschirm projezierte Phantasiewelt Hollywoods oder die elektronische Welt des Internets. Kinoliebhaber mag das Ambiente dieses Apartments an die faszinierenden Szenen der Filme von Wong Kar-Wai erinnern.

Le célibataire propriétaire de l'appartement, un jeune et célèbre architecte de Hong Kong, habite ce petit 30 m². La flexibilité spatiale provient de multiples opérations de partitions, d'éclairages et de mobilier mobile. L'ouverture principale de la fenêtre de devant offre diverses vues sur le monde – à travers la fenêtre elle-même ou via l'écran de cinéma panoramique sur le monde de fantaisie de Hollywood ou le cyber-monde d'Internet. L'atmosphère de l'appartement peut rappeler aux cinéphiles des scènes fascinantes des films de Wong Kar-Wai.

El propietario de este apartamento, un famoso y joven arquitecto de Hong Kong, habita un espacio reducido de 30 m². Gracias al funcionamiento variado y múltiple de las mamparas, a la iluminación y al mobiliario móvil se consigue crear un espacio flexible y abierto. La apertura central de la ventana que da a la calle ofrece diversas panorámicas, ya se trate de vistas reales del exterior como también, a través de su gigantesca pantalla, de imágenes del mundo fantasioso de Hollywood u otros campos. El ambiente que en él se respira bien podría evocar a los amantes del cine las películas de Wong Kar-Wai.

Architect: **e'vision (architects & associates) ltd.**

Location: **Shenzhen – China**

Eureka

Photographer: **e'vision** Completion date: **2001**

E ureka is a small flat located in Shenzhen built as a second home in which the owners can relax and entertain guests. e'vision's design for this small 600 sq. ft. flat apartment in the Eureka residential complex near the Lo Wo border is an example of how every inch of a restricted space can be exploited to the utmost. As the home has been designed for spending weekends and entertaining business contacts, a sense of fun and exuberance was the main feature of the simple brief. The architects put up a small wall between the hallway and the living space, to avoid the bad Feng Shui that arose when visitors found themselves facing directly on to the terrace.

E ureka ist ein kleines als Zweitwohnung konzipiertes Apartment in Shenzen, in dem die Eigentümer entspannen und Gäste empfangen können. e'visions Entwurf für das 55 m² große Apartment im Eureka Wohnkomplex nahe der Grenze zu Lo Wo verdeutlicht, wie ein begrenzter Raum optimal genutzt werden kann. Da es hauptsächlich für Wochenend-aufenthalte und die Unterhaltung von Geschäftsfreunden gedacht ist, sollte vor allem eine scherzhafte und überschwängliche Atmosphäre geschaffen werden. Die Architekten errich-teten eine Wand zwischen Wohnzimmer und Eingangsbereich, um negative Einflüsse des Feng Shui zu vermeiden, wenn die Gäste mit dem Gesicht zur Terrasse sitzen.

Eureka est un petit appartement de Shenzhen prévu pour le plaisir et les loisirs. Le design de e'vision pour ce 55 m² du complexe résidentiel Eureka à Shenzhen, près de la frontière de Lo Wo border, explore toutes les potentialités d'une petite résidence. Le lieu étant prévu pour les week end et la diversion des relations d'affaires, une sensation de plaisir et d'exubérance s'inscrivait en filigrane dans la commande. L'entrée contraire au Feng Shui, car face au balcon, a amené les architectes à créer un petit mur séparant l'espace de séjour du foyer.

Eureka es un pequeño apartamento ubicado en la ciudad de Shenzhen concebido por sus propietarios como segunda residencia para disfrutar y agasajar a sus invitados. El diseño por parte del estudio e'vision de este minúsculo espacio de 55 m² situado en la zona residencial de Eureka, cerca de la frontera de Lo Wo, constituye un verdadero ejercicio en las artes de explorar todo lo que un piso de reducidas dimensiones puede dar de sí. Al haber sido ideado para pasar fines de semana y extender invitaciones a contactos profesionales, se vislumbra un trasfondo de diversión y exuberancia. Los arquitectos colocaron una pequeña pared entre el vestíbulo y el espacio dedicado a vivienda, debido al mal feng shui que se producía cuando los visitantes quedaban orientados directamente hacia la terraza.

Architect: **Original Vision Limited**

Location: **Hong Kong – China**

Open Living

Photographer: **Kudos Photographic Design** Completion date: **1999**

Originally built in the 1970s, the architect's brief was to transform the house and make it as open, light and airy as possible. The atrium became the reference point for all the spaces, with the wall behind it providing the main focus with a waterfall and a sculpture. The owner's suite has been placed on the second floor; after removing all the non-structural walls, the sunlight can flood in and the sea is readily visible, particularly from the master bedroom and the bathroom area. The roof has become the setting for an open-air terrace, with a thermal bath and a barbecue area.

Der Auftrag des Architekten lautete, das in den 1970er Jahren erbaute Haus so offen, hell und transparent wie möglich zu gestalten. Das Atrium ist der Ausgangspunkt für die restlichen Räume des Hauses, wobei der Blick als erstes auf die Rückwand mit dem Wasserfall und der Skulptur gelenkt wird. Im zweiten Stock befindet sich die durch Beseitigung aller Trennwände lichtdurchflutete Suite des Eigentümers, deren Meeresblick vor allem vom Schlaf-und Badezimmer gewährleistet ist. Auf dem Dach befindet sich ein Dachgarten mit Thermalbadewanne und Grillterrasse.

L'architecte devait rendre cette construction des années 1970 aussi ouverte, claire et aérée que possible. L'atrium s'offre en référence à tous les espaces. Son mur arrière devient son épicentre, avec sa cascade et sa sculpture. Le second accueille une suite pour le propriétaire. Le retrait des murs non structurels inonde l'intérieur de lumière naturelle tout en offrant des vues sur la mer, spécialement dans la chambre principale et le bain. Sur le toit un jardin paysager a été aménagé doté d'un bain thermal et d'une terrasse barbecue.

Construida inicialmente durante los años setenta, el arquitecto tenía como misión transformar dicha casa en un espacio lo más abierto, claro y aireado posible. El atrio es el punto de referencia para el área de la vivienda. La pared posterior al mismo se convierte en su epicentro con una cascada de agua y una escultura. En el segundo piso se halla la suite del propietario. Al haber eliminado todos los tabiques no estructurales, el resultado es un espacio con abundante luz natural y con vistas al mar, en especial desde el dormitorio principal y el área de aseo. Sobre el tejado destaca la azotea al aire libre con su bañera termal y su terraza-barbacoa.

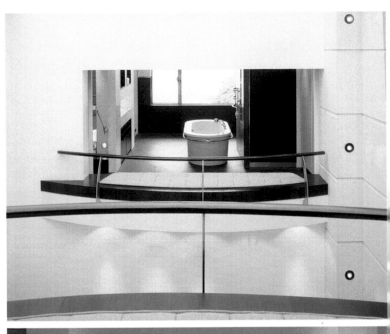

Architect: **Gary Chang – Edge Design Institute Ltd.**

Location: **Beijing – China**

Suitcase House

Photographer: **Satoshi Asakawa, Howard Chang, Gary Chang**

Completion date: **2001**

Suitcase House was created for the development project known as "The Commune by The Great Wall". Questioning the general image of a house, Suitcase House attempts to rethink the nature of intimacy, privacy, spontaneity and flexibility. It is a simple demonstration of the desire for maximum adaptability, in pursuit of a proscenium for infinite scenarios, of a plane of sensual pleasure. All the main areas inside the house provide good views of the Great Wall, as well as, obviously, the open terrace on the roof.

Das im Rahmen des Urbanisationsprojektes „The Commune by The Great Wall" entstandene und die herkömmliche Idee eines Hauses in Frage stellende Suitcase House versucht die Bedeutung von Intimität, Privatsphäre, Spontanität und Flexibilität erneut zu überdenken. Der Wunsch nach optimaler Anpassung kommt hier in der Suche nach einer Bühne für unendlich viele Szenarien, einer Spielwiese für sinnliche Vergnügen zum Ausdruck. Von allen wichtigen Räumen des Hauses hat man einen hervorragenden Blick auf die Chinesische Mauer, ebenso wie selbstverständlich von der offenen Dachterrasse.

Lancé à l'occasion du projet de développement « The Commune by The Great Wall », et interrogative sur l'image proverbiale de la maison, Suitcase House essaye de repenser la nature de l'intimité, de la vie privée, de la spontanéité et de la flexibilité. C'est une simple démonstration du désir d'adaptabilité ultime, l'avant-scène d'une infinité de scénarios, un plan de plaisir sensuel. Chacun des espaces principaux de la demeure offre de belles vues de la Grande Muraille, sans oublier, bien sûr, la terrasse du toit, complètement libre.

Nacido con motivo del proyecto de urbanización "The Commune by The Great Wall" (La Comuna junto a la Gran Muralla) e interrogándose sobre la imagen proverbial de la casa, Suitcase House trata de reconsiderar la naturaleza de la intimidad, la espontaneidad y de la flexibilidad. Es una simple muestra del deseo de máxima capacidad de adaptación, en la búsqueda de un proscenio para escenarios infinitos, un nivel de placer sensual. Los espacios principales del interior de la vivienda ofrecen magníficas vistas de la Gran Muralla, sin olvidar, por supuesto, la que se consigue desde la terraza abierta en lo alto del tejado.

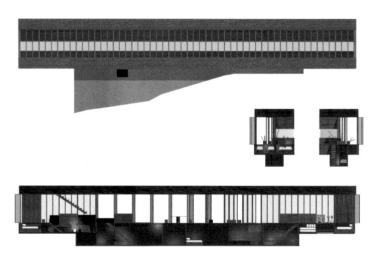

Section and elevation

Architect: **KNTA Architects**

Location: **Beijing – China**

The Twins for The Commune by The Great Wall

Photographer: **Satoshi Asakawa**   Completion date: **2002**

KNTA Architects is one of the most representative architectural studios in Singapore, and it is renowned throughout South-East Asia. According to KNTA, this house was designed to seamlessly blend into its natural surroundings. The layout, with one large building and a smaller annex, both of them L-shaped, and the careful positioning of the building in the valley help to create this integration. The annex, which houses the kitchen and the dining area, is tucked into the northern part of the valley, backing up against a steep precipice, and it is set at an angle of 45 degrees to the main building, which contains the living areas.

KNTA Architects ist eines der repräsentativsten Architekturbüros Singapurs und in ganz Südostasien anerkannt. Der Entwurf sollte das Haus laut KNTA nahtlos in seine natürliche Umgebung integrieren. Die aus einem größeren Gebäude und einem kleineren Anbau – beide L-förmig – bestehende Struktur dieses Hauses und seine sorgsame Platzierung im Tal haben zu dieser geglückten Integration beigetragen. Der Anbau, in dem sich Küche und Essraum befinden, schmiegt sich an einen steilen Abhang auf der Nordseite des Tales und steht im Winkel von 45 Grad zu dem Hauptgebäude, das die Wohn-und Schlafräume beherbergt.

KNTA Architects est l'un des cabinets d'architecture les plus représentatif et réputé de Singapour et du Sud-Est asiatique. Pour ce projet, selon KNTA, la demeure a été pensée pour s'intégrer parfaitement au cadre naturel. La conformation de la maison, un grand édifice et une annexe plus petite, tous deux en L, et leur disposition dans la vallée les accueillant ont aussi participé à cette intégration. L'annexe comprenant cuisine et aires de repas se niche contre une falaise, au nord de la vallée, à un angle de 45 degrés avec le corps principal, hébergeant les espaces de vie.

KNTA Architects es uno de los talleres de arquitectura más acreditados y representativos de Singapur y la región del sudeste asiático. En este proyecto, según ellos mismos, la vivienda ha sido diseñada para integrarse a la perfección en su contexto natural. El diseño, con un gran edificio junto a un pequeño anexo, ambos en forma de L, y la esmerada ubicación en el valle ayudaron a crear dicha integración. El anexo, que alberga la cocina y el área del comedor, está enclavado hacia la parte norte del valle, recostándose en un empinado precipicio, y formando un ángulo de 45 grados orientado hacia el edificio principal que acoge el área destinada a vivienda.

Architect: **Ai Wei Wei**

Location: **Beijing – China**

Ai Wei Wei's House

Photographer: **Satoshi Asakawa** Completion date: **1999**

The artist Ai Wei Wei was born in Beijing and lived and worked in New York from 1981 to 1993. He designed his own 5,300 sq. ft. house, which also serves him as a studio. Located in a village near the capital, it consists of a concrete structure—left exposed in the interior—with redbrick panels. Outside, this structure is clad with gray bricks and broken up by a few, meticulously calculated windows. The project is dominated by the two-stories that make up the artist's studio, set at right angles to the living section. This windowless studio only receives daylight from above, via two narrow skylights. In the artist's own words, it is a space where tradition and innovation efficently intersect.

Der aus Peking stammende Künstler Ai Wei Wei lebte und arbeitete zwischen 1981 und 1993 in New York. Das in einem Dorf nahe der Hauptstadt gelegene 500 m² große Haus hat er selbst entworfen und es dient ihm gleichzeitig als Atelier. Es besteht aus einem Rahmen aus Stahlbeton – innen unverkleidet gelassen – mit Paneelen aus rötlichen Ziegelsteinen. Von außen mit grauem Ziegel verkleidet, wurden einige umsichtig proportionierte Fensteröffnungen eingelassen. Hauptelement dieses Entwurfes ist das zweistöckige, fensterlose Künstleratelier, welches sich im rechten Winkel zum Wohntrakt befindet und nur durch zwei Oberlichter in der Decke mit Tageslicht versorgt wird. Der Künstler definiert ihn als einen Raum, in dem Tradition und Moderne wirkungsvoll miteineinander verwoben sind.

L'artiste Ai Wei Wei est né à Beijing et a vécu et travaillé à New York de 1981 à 1993. Il a conçu sa propre maison de 500 m², lui servant aussi d'atelier. Située dans un village proche de la capitale, elle repose sur une structure en béton armé – apparent à l'intérieur – avec des panneaux de brique rouge. La structure est revêtue à l'extérieur de briques grises, s'articulant avec quelques ouvertures de fenêtre dimensionnées avec soin. L'élément principal est l'espace atelier de l'artiste, sur deux niveaux, à angle droit du lieu de vie. Sans fenêtre, l'étude reçoit la lumière du jour uniquement via deux fines tabatières. Un espace d'intersection réelle de la tradition et de la nouveauté, selon l'artiste.

Ai Wei Wei es un artista nacido en Pekín que vivió y trabajó en Nueva York de 1981 a 1993. Ha diseñado su propia vivienda, de 500 m², que le sirve también como estudio. Ubicada en un pueblo cerca de la capital, consiste en una estructura de hormigón –dejada al descubierto en su interior– con paneles de ladrillo rojizos. Un revestimiento de ladrillo gris cubre el exterior de dicha estructura junto con unas pocas y minuciosamente calculadas ventanas. El elemento principal del proyecto es el espacio que forma el estudio de dos pisos, en una perspectiva adecuada a la extensión del salón. Sin ventanas, este estudio se alimenta de la luz solar a través de sus dos estrechas claraboyas. En palabras del propio artista, éste es un espacio donde lo tradicional y lo novedoso se entrecruzan eficazmente.

Architect: **Kanika R'kul – Leigh & Orange (Thailand) Ltd.**

Location: **Bangkok – Thailand**

he Shared House for The Commune by The Great Wall

Photographer: **Satoshi Asakawa**   Completion date: **2002**

Kanika R'kul is a talented young architect who is based in Bangkok but works elsewhere in Thailand, as well as overseas. According to the architect, although China has now entered into the modern world, the idea of a second home for weekends is still considered something new, a luxury for the elite. This house is set on a symbolically strong site, in a mountain range that may be visually inspiring but it is also physically daunting. The house comes to terms with the setting through its use of scale, form, orientation and placement of openings. Different parts of the house provide distinct perceptions of the space, according to the area and the scale. The house is approached as sequences of space that are not intended to be understood at first sight. Each space offers an encounter between the man-made and the natural.

Kanika R'kul, eine junger talentierte Architektin in Bangkok, deren Wirkungskreis sich über Thailand hinaus bis ins Ausland erstreckt, weist darauf hin, dass selbst im modernen China die Idee eines Wochenendhauses noch ungewöhnlich, luxuriös und privilegiert erscheint. Das Baugelände dieses Hauses besitzt symbolische Kraft, die Bergkette ist sowohl visuell inspirierend, als auch physisch eine Herausforderung, der das Gebäude durch Maßstab, Form, Ausrichtung und Transparenz gerecht wird. Von einzelnen Teilen des Hauses aus werden unterschiedliche Raumeindrücke vermittelt, je nach Gelände und Maßstab. Das Haus ist als Sequenz von Räumen konzipiert, die nicht auf den ersten Blick verstanden werden müssen. Jeder Raum stellt eine Begegnung von Bearbeitetem und Natur dar.

Kanika R'kul est un jeune et talentueux architecte d'avenir, basé à Bangkok mais aux ambitions globales, en Thaïlande et ailleurs. Selon lui, bien que la Chine entre dans une ère de modernité, l'idée de résidence secondaire reste un privilège nouveau, luxueux et un privilège. Le site accueillant la maison est symboliquement fort. La chaîne montagneuse est une inspiration visuelle et un défi physique. La demeure s'adapte au site via la dimension, la forme, l'orientation et le placement des ouvertures. Des divers espaces intérieurs, le site est perçu selon différentes portions et échelles. La maison est entendue comme des séquences spatiales ne devant pas être comprises dans l'instant. Chaque espace offre une rencontre entre l'artefact et la nature.

Kanika R'kul es una joven arquitecta de talento, natural de Bangkok, activa y con proyectos tanto en Tailandia como en el extranjero. Según ella, aunque China haya entrado ya en la era moderna, el ideal de poder poseer una casa de fin de semana se ve todavía como un concepto nuevo, como un lujo para privilegiados. El emplazamiento en el que se halla ubicada esta vivienda tiene una gran simbología. La cordillera montañosa sirve de inspiración a la vista a la vez que constituye un desafío desde el punto de vista físico. La casa trata el lugar mediante la escala, la forma, la orientación y la situación de claros. Desde diversos puntos de la vivienda se percibe en diferentes partes y escalas. La vivienda se concibe como una serie de secuencias, de espacios que no tienen por qué ser comprendidos al instante. Cada área ofrece un encuentro entre lo artificial y lo natural.

Architect: **Yung Ho Chang – Atelier Feichang Jianzhu**

Location: **Beijing – China**

Villa Shanyujian

Photographer: **Xing Fu**   Completion date: **1998**

The starting point for this country house was the desire to disrupt the existing terraced farmland as little as possible, while at the same time achieve the greatest possible interaction with the surrounding mountains and water, and the landscape in general. This initial concept led to a large roof, supported by a steel frame, which floats over the site as if it were a conceptual reconstruction of the hillside. Underneath, an expanse open space is divided into different areas by means of box-walls or small constructions, recalling the residential works of Louis Kahn, while the large windows on all sides of the chalet allow its residents to enjoy the stunning landscape outside.

Der Entwurf dieses Landhauses wurde durch den Wunsch bestimmt, den Bau möglichst bruchlos in das terrassenförmige Weideland einzufügen und eine optimale Wechselwirkung zwischen den umliegenden Bergen, dem Wasser und der Landschaft zu schaffen. Diese Idee wurde durch ein großes Dach verwirklicht, das, durch einen Stahlrahmen gestützt, konzeptionell die Hügellandschaft nachbildet und über dem Grundstück schwebt. Die weitläufige Wohnfläche ist in Anlehnung an Louis Kahns Wohnarchitektur durch schachtelartige Wände und kleine Konstruktionen in mehrere Räume unterteilt. Durch eine großzügige Verglasung auf allen Seiten können die Bewohner die wunderbare Landschaft genießen.

Le design de cette maison de campagne s'initie avec le désir de minimiser l'impact sur les cultures en terrasse existantes tout en maximisant l'interaction avec les montagnes proches, l'eau et le paysage en général. L'idée initiale est matérialisée par un grand toit, soutenu par un cadre d'acier et flottant sur le site, reconstruction conceptuelle du flanc de colline. En dessous, un espace de vie continu est divisé en plusieurs zones par des parois de caisson/mini édifice, en écho aux travaux résidentiels de Louis Kahn. Alors que le superbe paysage naturelle est invité via d'amples baies vitrées sur chaque face de la villa.

La concepción de esta casa de campo parte del deseo de minimizar cualquier perjuicio a los bancales de labranza actualmente existentes, pero intentando al mismo tiempo conseguir la máxima interrelación con la montaña, el agua y el paisaje en general de su entorno. La idea original se concretó en un amplio tejado que descansa en un armazón de acero que flota por encima del lugar como si de la reconstrucción conceptual de la ladera se tratara. En la parte inferior, un amplio espacio abierto destinado a vivienda queda dividido en diversas zonas mediante muros-caja o miniconstrucciones que recuerdan a la obra residencial de Louis Kahn. Entretanto, las amplias vidrieras colocadas por todo el chalet invitan a sus residentes al disfrute de su maravilloso paisaje natural exterior.

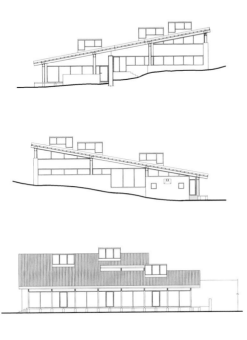

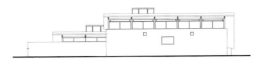

Section and elevation

Architect : **Chien Hsueh-Yi**

Location: **Beijing – China**

Airport

Photographer: **Satoshi Asakawa** Completion date: **2002**

According to Chien Hsueh-Yi, the architect who designed Airport, his main aim was to respect the history of the site, which has special historical and environmental significance, and design a structure that would harmoniously merge with its natural surroundings. The building's most striking feature is the stone wall, which follows the contours of the sloping terrain, setting up a remarkable contrast with the steep gradient. The wall is made of stone collected from the area, making it resemble somewhat the Great Wall of China, but also suggesting the spinal column of a living creature.

Nach Chien Hsueh-Yi, dem Architekt, der Airport entworfen hat, war es sein Hauptziel, die Geschichte des Baugeländes zu respektieren, das eine besondere historische sowie landschaftliche Bedeutung hat, und eine Struktur zu entwerfen, die harmonisch mit seiner natürlichen Umgebung verschmilzt. Die den Konturen des abfallenden Geländes folgende Steinmauer ist das Hauptmerkmal dieses Gebäudes und steht im Kontrast zu dem steilen Abhang. Die Mauersteine sind vom Baugelände aufgesammelt, so dass sie sowohl Ähnlichkeit mit der Chinesischen Mauer als auch mit der Wirbelsäule eines Lebewesens hat.

Selon Chien Hsueh-Yi, l'architecte créateur d'Airport, son but principal était de respecter l'histoire du pays, en raison du signifiant historique et environnemental spécial du lieu et de penser une structure s'intégrant au cadre pour un retour à la nature. Le mur de pierre du terrain pentu de la parcelle est l'aspect le plus frappant de l'ensemble, contrastant remarquablement avec l'inclinaison prononcée du sol. Le mur est en pierres provenant du site même, le faisant ressembler un peu à la Grande muraille de Chine tout en suggérant l'épine dorsale d'un être vivant.

Según Chien Hsueh-Yi, el arquitecto diseñador de Airport, debido al especial significado histórico y medioambiental del lugar el principal objetivo fue respetar la historia del terreno y diseñar una estructura que se integrase en la naturaleza en armonía con el hábitat. El aspecto más llamativo del edificio es su muralla de piedra, pegada al terreno en declive del solar y en fuerte contraste con la pronunciada pendiente del suelo. La muralla ha sido construida con piedra de la zona, lo cual confiere a la misma un cierto parecido con la Gran Muralla China, pero recordando también a la columna vertebral de una criatura viviente.

Architect: **Antonio Ochoa – Soho China Ltd.**

Location: **Bejing – China**

Cantilever House

Photographer: **Satoshi Asakawa** Completion date: **2002**

According to Beijing-based architect Antonio Ochoa, the Cantilever House embodies Yin and Yang. Yin because it was conceived for wintertime, is closed and feminine and is enhanced by the shade. Yang because it opens up to the landscape, harmoniously blends with the light and is masculine. Hot and cold, light and shadow, "time for plenitude and time for decrepitude, one side dragon and one side snake, like life itself", one time Yin, another Yang. The house stands virile on the mountain, between rocks and trees, hard and haughty. Inside it is like a lady: erotic, sensual, warm and lucid, charming, gentle, efficient and rational.

In dem Cantilever House erfüllen sich laut des in Peking arbeitenden Architekten Antonio Ochoa die Prinzipien des Yin und Yang. Yin, weil es, geschlossen und feminin, für den Winter konzipiert ist und der Schatten ihm noch zusätzlichen Glanz verleiht. Yang, weil es sich der Landschaft öffnet, mit dem Licht verschmilzt und maskulin ist. Wärme und Kälte, Licht und Schatten, „Zeit des Überflusses und des Verfalls, einerseits Drachen, andererseits Schlange, wie das Leben selbst" einmal Yin, ein anderes Mal Yang. Das Haus steht männlich potent auf dem Berg, zwischen Felsen und Bäumen, hart und arrogant. In seinem Inneren ist es wie eine Frau: erotisch, sinnlich, warm und offen, charmant, sanft, effizient und rational.

Selon l'architecte Antonio Ochoa, basé à Beijing, Cantilever House est Yin et Yang. Yin car pensée pour l'hiver, fermée, féminine et embellie par les ombres. Yang car ouverte sur le paysage, se mêlant à la lumière et masculin. Chaud et froid, ombre et lumière, « le temps de la plénitude et le temps de la décrépitude, une face dragon et l'autre serpent comme la vie », une fois Yin, l'autre Yang. La maison s'affiche virile sur la montagne, entre pierres et arbres, dure et hautaine. L'intérieur est une femme : érotique, sensuelle, chaleureuse et ample, douce, efficace et rationnelle.

Para Antonio Ochoa, arquitecto del proyecto y residente en Pekín, la Cantilever House representa el Yin y el Yang. El Yin porque ha sido concebida para invierno, es cerrada y femenina y la sombra le da realce. El Yang porque se abre al paisaje, se funde armónicamente con la luz y es masculina. Frío y caliente, luces y sombras, "ora plenitud, ora deterioro, por una parte dragón y por otra serpiente, como la vida misma", una vez Yin, la otra Yang. La casa se muestra viril en la montaña, entre rocas y árboles, dura y altiva. Por dentro es como una dama: erótica, sensual, cálida y despejada, encantadora, suave, eficiente y racional.

Architect: **Yung Ho Chang – Atelier Feichang Jianzhu**

Location: **Beijing – China**

Split House

Photographer: **Satoshi Asakawa** Completion date: **2002**

This house is "split" right down the middle to create various angles and spaces. According to its main architect, Yung Ho Chang, it also provides the sensation of lying "between mountains and rivers". Strikingly adaptable, with a design geared to the surrounding landscape, the two wings of the house can be placed anywhere from 0 to 360 degrees from each other, in order to adapt to the local terrain. The "Split House", an ecologically coherent earth and wood structure, respects Chinese tradition but does not attempt to recreate it; instead, it seeks to create a new architectural vision for a modern China.

Die direkt in der Mitte vorgenommene Spaltung dieses Hauses lässt verschiedene Winkel und Räume entstehen. Laut des verantwortlichen Architekten Yung Ho Chang soll es die Existenz „zwischen den Bergen und Flüssen" erfahrbar machen. Extrem anpassungsfähig mit einem Design, welches sich völlig in seine Umgebung einfügt, können die beiden Flügel des Hauses je nach Bedarf im beliebigen Winkel zwischen 0 bis 360 Grad plaziert werden. Das „Split House" zollt mit seiner ökologischen Strukur aus Holz und Erde der chinesischen Bautradition Respekt, ohne sie wiederbeleben zu wollen. Eher präsentiert es eine neue architektonische Vision für das moderne China.

La maison est divisée par le milieu pour créer divers angles et espaces. Selon son principal architecte, Yung Ho Chang, elle offre aussi un sens de l'existence « entre montagne et rivière ». Étonnamment adaptable et flexible, son design peut s'adapter à la topographie environnante. Ses deux ailes peuvent être placées partout de 0 à 360 degrés l'une de l'autre, pour accommoder le terrain avoisinant. La « Split House », une structure écologique saine, en bois et en terre, représente le respect de la tradition chinoise sans chercher à la recréer. C'est plutôt une nouvelle vision architecturale pour une Chine moderne.

La Split House se divide justo por la mitad para crear varios ángulos y espacios. Tal como ha comentado su arquitecto principal, Yung Ho Chang, provoca una sensación de estar entre montañas y ríos. Profundamente versátil, con un diseño que se adapta a la topografía del medio, las dos alas de la casa pueden colocarse en cualquier posición, de los 0 a los 360 grados de separación entre ellas, a fin de adaptarse al terreno circundante. La Split House, con un armazón profundamente ecológico de madera y tierra, mantiene el respeto por la tradición arquitectónica de China, aunque no persigue una recreación de ésta. Más bien se trata de un intento de crear una nueva visión arquitectónica para una nueva China.

Architect: **Kengo Kuma**

Location: **Beijing – China**

Bamboo Wall

Photographer: **Satoshi Asakawa**   Completion date: **2002**

This is a villa designed by the renowned Japanese architect Kengo Kuma for "The Commune by The Great Wall" project. His first step was an in-depth study of the formal characteristics of the Great Wall. He claims that the fascination this monument exerts could be seen as a veiled criticism of conventional forms of architecture, which often seek to create an isolated object enclosed within its own habitat. Then, Kengo Kuma tried to apply the features of the Great Wall that he most admired to this domestic setting and, to emphasize this, the house is known simply as the "Wall". The architect chose to use bamboo as the main material, due to its primordial importance in both Chinese and Japanese culture.

Dieses Landhaus wurde von dem bekannten japanischen Architekten Kengo Kumo im Rahmen des Projektes „The Commune by The Great Wall" entworfen. Zunächst studierte er genauestens die Form und Gestalt der Chinesischen Mauer. Die Faszination, die dieses Monument ausübt, kann, behauptet der Architekt, auch als Kritik an die konventionellen Formen der Architektur verstanden werden, die mehr und mehr ihre Umgebung außer Acht lassend zum Selbstzweck geraten. Aus diesem Grunde wollte Kengo Kuma die Charakteristika der Chinesischen Mauer in das Wohnhaus mit einfließen lassen. Um dies zu unterstreichen, wird von dem Haus einfach als die „Mauer" gesprochen. Bambus, bedeutungsreich sowohl in der chinesischen als auch japanischen Kultur, ist hier vorherrschendes Baumaterial.

Cette villa a été conçue pour le projet « The Commune by The Great Wall » par le célèbre architecte japonais Kengo Kuma. Initialement, il souhaitait étudier et en savoir plus sur la formalité de la Grande muraille. Son intérêt pouvait aussi être compris comme une critique de la forme architecturale conventionnelle, tendant à devenir un objet isolé au sein de son habitat. Il souhaitait diffuser les propriétés de la Grande muraille dans l'acte résidentiel. De ce fait, il est seulement référé à la maison comme « Muraille ». L'architecte a choisit comme matière primale le bambou, un véhicule très signifiant pour les cultures chinoises et japonaises.

Este chalet fue diseñado para el proyecto conjunto "The Commune by The Great Wall" (La Comuna junto a la Gran Muralla) por el arquitecto japonés Kengo Kuma, quien se propuso estudiar y profundizar en las características formales de la Gran Muralla. La fascinación que ésta despertaba se podía entender, según el arquitecto, como una velada crítica a las formas convencionales de la arquitectura en sí, que tiende a convertirse en un objeto aislado de su propio hábitat. Kengo Kuma intentó aplicar a esta vivienda las propiedades y características que aprecia en la Gran Muralla. Para enfatizarlo, la casa es conocida como La Muralla. Debido a la relevancia de que goza en ambas culturas, china y japonesa, el arquitecto optó por utilizar el bambú como material principal.

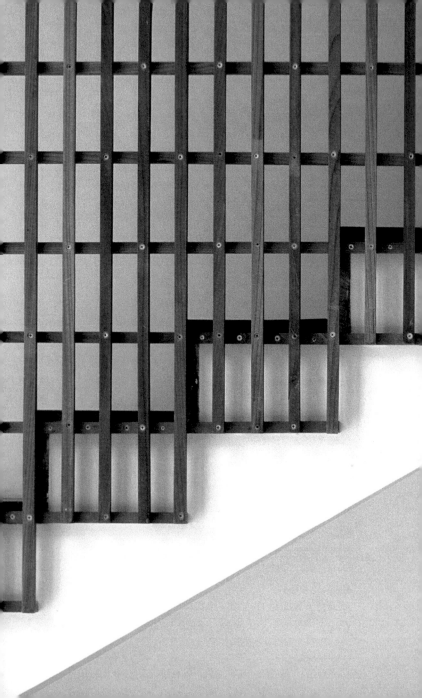

Architect: **Studio Nasca – Nobuaki Furuya**

Location: **Beijing – China**

Forest House

Photographer: **Satoshi Asakawa** Completion Date: **2002**

The Forest House is another holiday home designed as part of the complex known as "The Commune by The Great Wall". This house, seemingly scooped out of the mountain, gives the impression that it is permanently enshrouded by the forest. Although the architects used commonplace local materials, their skilful exploitation of innovative building techniques has resulted in a highly unusual environment. All the rooms feature a series of vertical slits, so their occupants can glimpse different views as they move around inside the house, setting up continuous interactions between the architecture, the topography and the forest.

Forest House ist ein weiteres Landhaus, welches im Rahmen des Projektes „The Commune by The Great Wall" entworfen wurde. Scheinbar aus dem Berg modelliert, vermittelt das Haus das Gefühl, jederzeit von Wald umgeben zu sein. Durch neue Bauweisen wurde ein außergewöhnlicher Raum geschaffen, auch wenn die Architekten auf ganz gewöhnliche und in der Gegend herkömmliche Baumaterialen zurückgriffen. Aufgrund der sich durch alle Räume ziehenden vertikalen Verstrebung bieten sich dem Bewohner beim Durchschreiten der einzelnen Zimmer verschiedene Panoramen der Außenwelt. So wird eine ständige Wechselwirkung zwischen Architektur, Topographie und Wald erfahrbar.

Forest House est une autre résidence de vacance du projet « The Commune by the Great Wall ». Dans la maison, sculptée dans la montagne, la sensation d'encerclement par les bois est permanente. Malgré l'emploi de matériaux ordinaires pour le projet, les architectes ont créé un espace extraordinaire grâce aux méthodes de construction innovantes. Chaque pièce intégrant des fentes verticales répétées, les occupants peuvent visualiser différentes scènes selon l'endroit de la maison, changeantes à mesure de leurs déplacements. Les résidents peuvent ainsi modifier leurs expériences en séquences organisées, mais c'est aussi le début d'interactions continues entre l'architecture, la topographie et la forêt.

Forest House es otra casa de campo diseñada para el proyecto "The Commune by The Great Wall". Casi extraída de las entrañas de la montaña, sus moradores tienen la sensación de estar siempre rodeados de bosque. Aunque se utilizaron materiales corrientes en la zona, el extraordinario resultado se debe a la pericia de los arquitectos en el uso de métodos de construcción novedosos. Al disponer todas las habitaciones una serie de rendijas verticales, se pueden visualizar diferentes vistas del exterior a medida que se van moviendo por la casa. Se crean así continuas interacciones entre arquitectura, topografía y paisaje.

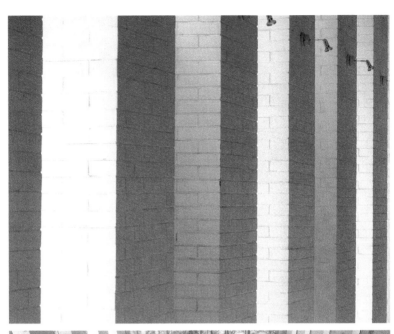

Architect: **Ray Chen – JRV International Co. Ltd.**

Location: **Taipei – Taiwan**

Mr. Ho: Project 1

Photographer: **W. M. Ruen** Completion date: **2002**

Attracted by the reputation of Ray Chen, the owner of this house decided to dramatically change the style of his home. He asked for a house that would serve as both a work space and a residence, as, at the age of nearly sixty, he still relishes his work. Pat Huang has noted in Interior Magazine, that the first floor of this typical narrow, deep townhouse now contains the owner's office, while the upper part provides the family's living quarters. These are dominated by the dining area, with sunlight pouring through its enormous windows, while a small, discreet recess serves as the master bedroom. Finally, a tiny third floor houses just one bedroom, although this gives on to a roof garden floored with wooden planks. A large soundproof window is carefully arranged to frame a view of the mountain, while also managing to keep the chaos of the urban sprawl out of sight.

Der gute Ruf von Ray Chen veranlasste den knapp 60jährigen und noch voll im Berufsleben stehenden Eigentümer dieses Hauses, eine radikale Erneuerung seiner Wohnstätte vornehmen zu lassen, um in ihr Arbeits- und Wohnräume zu vereinigen. Pat Huang erklärt im Interior Magazine , dass sich nun im ersten Stock dieses typischen schmalen und tiefen Stadthauses das Büro des Besitzers befindet, während im oberen Teil die Privaträume liegen, wie das durch eine große Fensterfront lichtdurchflutete Esszimmer und das in einer schmalen Kammer untergebrachte Schlafzimmer des Besitzers. Ein weiteres Schlafzimmer und ein mit Holzbohlen ausgelegter Dachgarten befinden sich in dem räumlich begrenzten dritten Stock. Ein sorgsam eingelassenes, schalldichtes großes Fenster zeigt auf einen Berg, während der Blick auf die chaotische Stadtlandschaft ausgespart bleibt.

Attiré par la réputation de Ray Chen, le propriétaire a décidé de changer spectaculairement son type de résidence. Approchant les 60 ans et toujours heureux de travailler, il a souhaité que sa maison serve à la fois d'espace de vie et de travail. Comme indiqué par Pat Huang dans Interior Magazine, le premier niveau de cette maison urbaine typique, étroite et longue, accueille le bureau du propriétaire le haut étant dédié à la vie de famille. L'aire des repas, illuminée naturellement par des baies translucides du sol au plafond, domine cette partie de la maison. La chambre de maître se trouve dans une pièce étroite. Enfin, un tout petit troisième étage abrite une chambre et un toit paysager en parquet. Une grande fenêtre anti-bruit est disposée avec soin pour encadrer une montagne tout en cachant le chaos du paysage urbain.

Atraído por el buen nombre de Ray Chen, el propietario de esta casa decidió cambiar radicalmente su tipo de vivienda. Aún disfrutando del trabajo a sus casi sesenta años, encomendó que le diseñaran una casa para vivir y trabajar. Tal como indica Pat Huang en "Interior Magazine", el primer piso de esta típica casa urbana larga y estrecha se ha reservado como oficina y la parte superior está dedicada a vivienda familiar. En ella destaca el comedor, con grandes ventanales translúcidos que permiten el paso de abundante luz solar. El dormitorio principal está en una angosta estancia. Por último, un tercer piso de reducidas dimensiones alberga una habitación y una azotea ajardinada con parquet. Un gran ventanal insonorizado colocado con esmero permite a sus inquilinos disfrutar de las vistas de la montaña, evitándoles al mismo tiempo la visión de una parte caótica del paisaje urbano.

251

Architect: **Ray Chen – JRV International Co. Ltd.**

Location: **Taipei – Taiwan**

Mr. Ho: Project 2

Photographer: **W. M. Ruen** Completion date: **2001**

This project was realized in an old neighborhood in the center of Taipei. The building's narrow, 13-foot facade contrasts with its depth of 65 feet. As the client also owned the neighboring building, the designer was free to incorporate part of this plot into the project. As Pat Huang has observed in Interior Magazine, the narrow existing staircase provides access to the home. The main floor contains the living room; a skylight in the center of the ceiling floods this space with abundant sunlight, while a spiral staircase links it to the dining room upstairs. The natural colors of wood imbue this house with a warm atmosphere.

Dieses Projekt wurde in einem alten Stadtviertel im Zentrum von Taipei realisiert. Die 4 m breite Fassade des Gebäudes kontrastiert mit seiner Tiefe von 20 m. Da dem Besitzer auch das anliegende Gebäude gehört, wurde es von dem Architekten in das Projekt miteinbezogen. Wie Pat Huang im Interior Magazine beschreibt, gewährt die schon vorhandene schmale Treppe Zugang zu der Wohnung und führt direkt in den ersten Stock, wo sich das Wohnzimmer befindet, welches durch ein Oberlicht mit viel Tageslicht versorgt wird. Von hier aus führt eine Wendeltreppe zu dem ein Stockwerk höher gelegenen Esszimmer. Natürliche Holztöne verleihen dem Haus eine warme Atmosphäre.

Le projet s'invite dans une ancien quartier du centre de Taipei. La façade de 4 m contraste avec une profondeur de 20 m. Le client possédant aussi l'édifice voisin, une partie a intégré ce projet, à la demande de l'architecte. Pat Huang décrivait dans Interior Magazine un étroit escalier existant offrant un accès direct à la demeure, menant au niveau principal où se découvrait un séjour avec une claire-voie au centre du plafond offrant une lumière naturelle abondante à cet espace. Un escalier en spirale le relie avec la salle à manger du haut. La couleur bois naturel offre une ambiance chaleureuse à l'endroit.

Este proyecto se llevó a cabo en un viejo barrio del centro de Taipei. La fachada de cuatro metros de ancho de este edificio contrasta con sus veinte de profundidad. Al ser el cliente también propietario del edificio contiguo, al diseñador se le permitió incorporar parte del solar vecino. Como Pat Huang dice en "Interior Magazine", se accede a la casa por las actuales y estrechas escaleras, y una vez en la planta principal el visitante llega al salón. Un tragaluz en la parte central del techo proporciona a este espacio grandes dosis de luz natural. El comedor, en la planta superior, se comunica con el salón mediante una escalera de caracol. El color de madera natural infunde un cálido ambiente a toda la vivienda.

Architect: **Seung, H-Sang – Iroje architects & planners**

Location: **Seoul – South Korea**

Sujol-dang

Photographer: **Satoshi Asakawa** Completion date: **1993**

Seung, H-Sang has become one of the most important contemporary architects in South Korea. His Sujol-dang project is a prime example of his architectural philosophy, which attempts to restore the ancient concept of space that has been lost in a flood of buildings that are wrongly considered Western and modern in style but are essentially mediocre. When designing this house, the architect asked himself whether he could establish a new typology for urban housing, how a building should connect with the urban fabric, whether it should be functional, and what is the relationship between the space and the lives of its inhabitants. Finally, the design for this house marked the beginning of a movement to create modern, original yet intellectual domestic architecture.

Seung, H-Sang ist einer der bedeutendsten zeitgenössischen Architekten in Südkorea. Sein Entwurf Sujol-dang ist ein erstklassiges Beispiel für seine architektonische Vision, die alte und leider inmitten einer Fülle von mittelmäßigen, fälschlicherweise als modern oder westlich bezeichneten Gebäuden verloren gegangene Idee von Raumerfahrung wiederherzustellen. Fragen nach einer neuen Typologie von urbanen Unterkünften, der Verbindung zwischen Wohnhaus und städtischer Struktur, der Funktionalität von Wohnhäusern und der Beziehung zwischen Lebensraum und Lebensweise bewegten den Architekten während der Konzeption dieses Hauses. Letztendlich markiert dieser Entwurf den Beginn einer Bewegung der modernen und originellen sowie intellektuellen Wohngestaltung.

Seung, H-Sang est devenu l'un des plus importants architectes contemporains en Corée du sud. Son projet, Sujol-dang, est exemplaire de sa pensée architecturale, reflétée dans ses tentatives de restaurer l'ancien esprit spatial perdu parmi l'ensemble des construction modernes, mais médiocres, à l'occidentalisme mal compris. Créant cette maison, l'architecte s'est demandé s'il pouvait établir une autre typologie du logement urbain, si un édifice devait être lié au tissu urbain, si la fonctionnalité était essentielle, quelle était la relation entre l'espace et la vie des habitants. À terme, le design de cette résidence a marqué le début d'un mouvement créatif du design de logement, moderne et original mais aussi intellectuel.

Seung, H-Sang es uno de los arquitectos contemporáneos más importantes de Corea del Sur. Sujol-dang es un ejemplo óptimo de su línea de pensamiento arquitectónico, en la que intenta reinstaurar el antiguo concepto de espacio perdido en medio de edificios erróneamente identificados como de corte occidental o modernos, aunque mediocres. Al diseñar Sujol-dang el arquitecto se preguntó cuestiones como si sería posible crear una nueva tipología de vivienda urbana, cómo debería un edificio enlazar con el tejido urbano, si la casa debería responder a criterios de funcionalidad o cuál es la relación entre el espacio y las vidas de sus habitantes. En último término, el diseño de Sujol-dang señaló el inicio de un movimiento caracterizado por un diseño moderno y original, y también intelectual, de la vivienda.

First floor

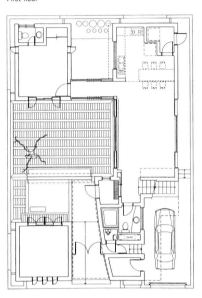

Section

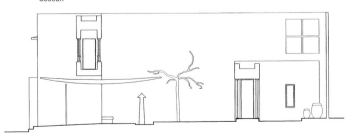

Architect: **Saurus**

Location: **Kyushu – Japan**

Booths

Photographer: **Satoshi Asakawa**   Completion date: **2000**

This four-story building is situated in Kagoshima, an area in southern Japan formerly known as Satsuma with a unique character and history. The first floor of the house contains the Saurus architectural studio. The second and third floors are apartments that provide lodging for young female students, while the fourth floor is where the owner and architect, Mr. Uto, lives with his family. The second and third floors are both lined with four booths, measuring 7 sq. ft. Each booth is a small private space for one student, while a spacious area in the middle is designed as a communal space that serves as kitchen, dining room and lounge.

Dieses vierstöckige Gebäude liegt in Kagoshima, früher unter dem Namen Satsuma bekannt, einer Gegend im Süden Japans mit einzigartiger Ausprägung und Geschichte. Im ersten Stock befindet sich das Architekturbüro Saurus. Die im zweiten und dritten Stock gelegenen Wohnungen dienen jungen Studentinnen als Unterkunft, während im vierten Stock der Eigentümer und Architekt, Herr Uto, mit seiner Familie wohnt. Im zweiten und dritten Stock befinden sich zu beiden Seiten vier jeweils 2 x 2 m große Zellen. Jede Zelle stellt einen kleinen privaten Raum für seine Bewohnerin dar, während ein in der Mitte gelegener größerer Bereich als gemeinschaftliche Küche, Ess-und Wohnzimmer dient.

Cet immeuble de quatre étages est à Kagoshima, au sud du japon, une région à la personnalité et à l'histoire uniques, l'ancienne Satsuma. Le premier niveau de la maison accueille l'atelier d'architecture Saurus. Le second et le troisième intègrent des appartements, les dortoirs de jeunes étudiantes, et le dernier étage abrite l'architecte et propriétaire, M. Uto, et sa famille. Quatre cabines de 2 x 2 m sont alignées par deux sur les côtés de chaque niveau intermédiaire. Chaque cabine est un espace privé pour chaque résident, une vaste zone centrale étant conçue comme un espace public commun servant de cuisine et de lieu de repas/séjour.

Este edificio de cuatro pisos está situado en Kagoshima, al sur de Japón, antigua Satsuma, una zona con historia y personalidad. El primer piso acoge el estudio de arquitectura Saurus. El segundo y el tercer pisos son apartamentos para chicas estudiantes, mientras que el cuarto está destinado a vivienda del propietario y arquitecto del inmueble y su familia, los Uto. En el segundo y tercer piso hay cuatro cabinas de 2 x 2 metros cada una puestas en fila a ambos lados, con la función de ser un pequeño reducto de privacidad para cada uno de sus inquilinos. Entretanto, en el centro converge un área espaciosa común que hace las funciones de cocina, comedor y salón.

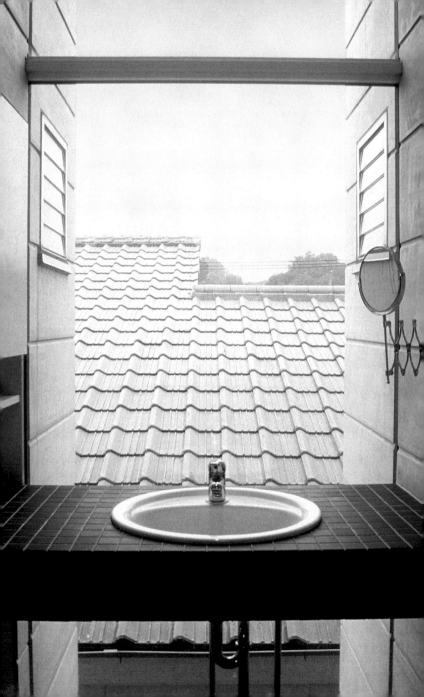

Architect: **Guen Bertheau-Suzuki**

Location: **Kyushu – Japan**

F-House

Photographer: **Seiichiro Otake** Completion date: **2002**

The owners of F-House, built on hills overlooking an extensive urban sprawl, can enjoy the natural scenery nearby from their charming wooden terrace. The lounge-dining room on the ground floor is set off by its large window connected to the outside terrace. The U-shape design of the building allows its occupants to enjoy the feeling of being in the open air without relinquishing their privacy. The double-glazed window on the southern face blocks out ultraviolet rays. All the rooms have been fitted with under-floor heating, and the lounge-dining room also boasts a 24-hour automatic ventilation system. The distinctive modern design of this Japanese-style room endows the house with a special charm.

Die Eigentümer des F-House, das auf den Hügeln über dem urbanen Getümmel steht, können die nahegelegene Natur von der bezaubernden Holzterrasse genießen. In dem im Parterre gelegenen Wohn-/Esszimmer fällt das große Fenster auf, das auf die Terrasse führt. Dank seiner U-förmigen Anlage bietet das Haus seinen Bewohnern sowohl Intimität als auch das Gefühl der Offenheit. Das nach Süden gerichtete Fenster besitzt eine mit UV-Filter ausgestattete Doppelverglasung, außerdem sind alle Räume mit Fußbodenheizung und das Wohn-/Esszimmer mit einem Tag und Nacht laufenden Belüftungssystem ausgestattet. Das ausgesuchte und moderne Design dieses Raumes im japanischen Stil verleiht dem Haus einen speziellen Charme.

Les propietaires de F-House, construite sur les collines surplombant une zone métropoli-taine, peuvent profiter de l'environnement naturel depuis leur charmante terrasse en bois. Le séjour, au rez-de-chaussée, est mis en valeur par sa grande baie vitrée connectée à la terrasse extérieure. Grâce au design en U, les occupants peuvent jouir de la sensation d'être à l'air libre tout en préservant leur intimité. Dotée d'un double vitrage intégrant un fil-tre anti UV au sud, chaque chambre a reçu un chauffage au sol. Un système de ventilation 24h/24 a également été incorporé au séjour. Le design unique et moderne des pièces de style japonais ajoute aussi un charme particulier au lieu.

Construida sobre unos cerros desde donde se domina una amplia zona urbana, los due-ños de F-House disfrutan del paisaje desde la agradable terraza construida en madera. Destaca del salón comedor, en la planta inferior, cuyo amplio ventanal conecta con la terra-za. Gracias al diseño en forma de U de este edificio, sus habitantes gozan de una sensa-ción de abertura al aire libre a la vez que se respeta su intimidad. Una ventana de doble cristal situada en la parte sur evita el paso de los rayos ultravioleta. Todas las habitaciones disponen de un sistema de calefacción bajo el pavimento. En el salón comedor se ha ins-talado también un sistema de ventilación automático las 24 horas del día. El original y moderno diseño de su habitación de estilo japonés confiere añadido encanto al conjunto.

Architect: **Guen Bertheau-Suzuki**

Location: **Kobe – Japan**

J-House

Photographer: **Nacása & Partners Inc.** Completion date: **1992**

The house is located on a hill with views of Kobe harbor. As its owners, a married couple, share their lives with 3 dogs, 2 cats and 1 parrot, they placed special emphasis on designing a space suited to their pets. The architects accomplished this by designing a semi-exterior room for the animals, easily visible from the lounge, dining room and kitchen. They consider that the most difficult part of the design process was their inability to discuss it with the other interested parties—the animals themselves. Nevertheless, it is hard to imagine these pets living in better conditions, especially after their own special space was fitted with a skylight and air conditioning.

Dieses auf einem Berg gelegene Haus mit Sicht auf den Hafen von Kobe wird von einem Ehepaar zusammen mit ihren 3 Hunden, 2 Katzen und 1 Papagei bewohnt. Die Aufgabe, einen eigenen Raum für die Haustiere zu konstruieren, lösten die Architekten mit dem Entwurf einer Art Wintergarten, der sowohl vom Wohn-und Esszimmer, als auch von der Küche zu überschauen ist. Das schwierigste Problem dabei war laut Ihnen die Unmöglichkeit, mit den Tieren selbst den Entwurf zu diskutieren. Trotz allem ist es schwer vorstellbar, dass die Tiere besser versorgt sein könnten als in diesem eigens für sie eingerichteten Raum mit Oberlicht und Klimaanlage .

La maison habite une colline permettant de contempler le port de Kobe. Les propriétaires, un couple marié, partageant le lieu avec 3 chiens, 2 chats et 1 perroquet, donc il fallait prévoir un espace adapté aux animaux. Les architectes ont pour ce faire conçu une pièce semi extérieure pour les animaux, facilement visible depuis le séjour, la salle à manger et la cuisine. Ils confessent pourtant que le point le plus difficile fut l'impossibilité de débattre du sujet avec les premiers intéressés. Cependant, en offrant une fenêtre en claire-voie et l'air conditionné à cette pièce, les animaux peuvent difficilement trouver de meilleures conditions durant toute l'année.

La casa se halla emplazada en lo alto de una colina desde donde se puede divisar el puerto de Kobe. Para el matrimonio propietario de esta vivienda revestía una especial importancia el diseño de un espacio adecuado para sus animales de compañía: 3 perros, 2 gatos y 1 loro. Los arquitectos satisficieron su deseo diseñando una estancia casi al aire libre para los animales fácilmente visible desde el comedor, el salón y la cocina. Según ellos, el elemento más difícil en la planificación fue no poder discutir los detalles con los propios interesados. Pese a todo, tras colocar un tragaluz e instalar aire acondicionado en este espacio reservado para ellos, podemos afirmar que viven en inmejorables condiciones.

Architect: **Guen Bertheau-Suzuki**

Location: **Hachijo Island, Tokyo – Japan**

Tsuruzono House

Photographer: **Nacása & Partners Inc.** Completion date: **2000**

This is a weekend house built for a painter and his wife, who live in the city of Tokyo. It is located in Hachijo, one of the seven islands of the Izu archipelago, some 185 miles south of the capital but still administratively attached to its prefecture. Hachijo can be reached by airplane from the Tokyo metropolitan area in 45 minutes, but it has a totally different atmosphere and climate from the metropolis. The owner of Tsuruzono House, whose main hobby is scuba diving, commissioned this project from the architect Guen Bertheau-Suzuki, who also loves going scuba diving in the area. The metal structure on display inside the house is not only there for esthetic reasons—part of it also responds to the need to keep rust under control, for maintenance purposes.

Dieses Wochenendhaus wurde für einen in Tokio lebenden Maler und seine Frau gebaut und befindet sich 300 km südlich der Hauptstadt auf Hachijo, einer der sieben Inseln des Izu-Archipels, 45 Flugminuten von Tokio entfernt, aber verwaltungstechnisch an sie angegliedert. In einer verglichen mit Tokio klimatisch und atmosphärisch völlig anderen Umgebung beauftragten die Eigentümer des Tsuruzono House, beide leidenschaftliche Sporttaucher, den Architekten und ebenfalls gerne in der Gegend tauchenden Guen Bertheau-Suzuki mit ihrem Projekt. Die Metallstruktur im Inneren des Hauses hat nicht nur ästhetische sondern auch praktische Gründe, nämlich dem Rost Einhalt zu gebieten.

La résidence secondaire construite pour un peintre et son épouse, résidents du centre de Tokyo. Située sur Hachijo, l'une des sept îles de l'archipel d'Izu, à 300 km au sud de la capitale mais rattachée à sa préfecture, l'île est à 45 minutes d'avion de la métropole tokyoïte. Elle jouit d'une atmosphère et d'un climat radicalement différents de ceux de Tokyo dont elle dépend. Le propriétaire, dont le hobby est la plongée, a confié ce projet à l'architecte Guen Bertheau-Suzuki, adepte lui aussi du monde sous-marin de la région. La structure métallique est visible dans la maison : une solution conceptuelle et une réponse aux besoins d'entretien, afin de contrôler la rouille.

Esta es una casa de fin de semana construida para un pintor y su esposa, residentes en Tokio. La casa se halla situada en Hachijo, una de las siete islas que conforman el archipiélago de las islas Izu, a 300 kilómetros y 45 minutos de avión del área metropolitana de Tokio. En esta isla, con un clima y ambiente general totalmente diferentes a la capital a la que pertenece administrativamente, el propietario de Tsuruzono House, gran amante del submarinismo, encargó el proyecto de la misma al arquitecto Guen Bertheau-Suzuki, también aficionado y practicante de este deporte en la zona. La estructura de metal visible en su interior responde no sólo a criterios puramente de diseño sino también a la necesidad de mantener bajo control, por cuestiones de mantenimiento, el fenómeno de la herrumbre.

Architect: **Toshiko Kawaguchi**

Location: **Tokyo – Japan**

Chez Moi

Photographer: **Nacása & Partners Inc.** Completion date: **2002**

This house is located in the center of Tokyo, near a ring road that is nearly always awash with heavy traffic. The extreme conditions of these surroundings, combined with the fact that the property is surrounded by buildings on three sides, has left the hemmed-in house with only one 13-foot-wide opening, on the north side, overlooking a street. Despite all these inconveniences, the architect has managed to come up with a very comfortable residence. The owner of this five-story building rents out the first two floors, but he has kept the remaining three floors for his own use. A stairwell in the center of the building provides access to his private floors, while also serving as a skylight and creating a striking optical effect.

Dieses Haus befindet sich, auf drei Seiten von anderen Gebäuden eingeschlossen, in der Nähe einer stark befahrenen Ringstraße im Zentrum von Tokio. Aufgrund dieser ungünstigen Lage besitzt das Haus nur eine nach Norden ausgerichtete 4 m weite Öffnung, die auf eine Straße geht. Trotz aller Nachteile gelang es dem Architekten, ein sehr komfortables Wohnhaus zu schaffen. Während die unteren zwei Etagen dieses fünfstöckigen Gebäudes vermietet sind, bewohnt der Eigentümer die restlichen drei Stockwerke. Die dorthin führende Treppe erstreckt sich in der Mitte des Gebäudes bis zu einem Oberlicht und dient auch als Blickfang.

La maison se situe au centre de Tokyo, près d'une rocade débordant de circulation. Les conditions environnantes peu favorables et l'encerclement par des buildings concèdent à cette demeure assiégée une simple ouverture de 4 m de large, au nord, face à la rue. En dépit de l'adversité, l'architecte a réussi une résidence très confortable. Alors que le premier et le deuxième niveaux de l'immeuble de cinq étages sont loués, le propriétaire occupe les trois derniers niveaux. Une cage d'escalier, accédant aux étages privés du propriétaire et située au centre de l'immeuble, offre non seulement un éclairage zénithal mais aussi un puit optique.

Esta casa está en el centro de Tokio, cerca de una de ronda de circunvalación, a rebosar casi siempre de tráfico. A causa de las extremas condiciones del entorno y el hecho de que la casa está rodeada de edificios por tres de sus cuatro costados, esta sitiada estructura tiene una sola abertura frontal de cuatro metros en su cara norte, que da a una calle. Pese a tal adversidad, el arquitecto consiguió crear una casa muy cómoda. En este edificio de cinco plantas, el propietario alquila los dos primeros pisos y mantiene para sí los tres superiores. El cubo de la escalera, en el centro, permite el acceso a las plantas del propietario, y además cumple la función de tragaluz y crea un precioso efecto óptico.

Architect: **Toshiko Kawaguchi**

Location: **Niigata – Japan**

Sano House

Photographer: **Katsuaki Furudate**   Completion date: **1997**

This house is located in the suburbs of Niigata city, next to a paddy field. It was designed for the owner of one of the area's most important businesses, who wanted it built for his wife as a present for having shared all the hard work that has made their business so prosperous. The architect bore in mind the wife's special request for a home devoid of any barriers, suitable for the coming years when they will be an elderly retired couple. The layout also had to cater to the needs of the various dogs and cats that live with the family. Kawaguchi used charcoal as the main material, thereby reclaiming ground from the paddy field and alleviating the effects of the humidity.

Dieses Haus wurde für einen Geschäftsinhaber in den Vororten der Stadt Niigata neben einem Reisfeld gebaut und seiner Ehefrau zum Geschenk gemacht, aus Dank für die Jahre harter Arbeit, die sie an seiner Seite während des Auf- und Ausbaus ihres heute florierenden Geschäftes verbrachte. Dem ausdrücklichen Wunsch der Hauseigentümerin, ein im Hinblick auf das zukünftige Rentenalter adäquates und leicht zugängliches Haus zu bauen, wurde von Seiten der Architektin Kawaguchi Genüge getan. Auch wurden in der Hausstruktur die in der Familie lebenden Hunde und Katzen mitberücksichtigt. Um auf einem ehemaligen Reisfeld bauen zu können und den Problemen der Feuchtigkeit beizukommen, benutzte Kawaguchi als Hauptmaterial Holzkohle.

Dans la banlieue de la ville de Niigata, cette maison s'invite auprès d'une rizière. Elle a été pensée pour le propriétaire d'un grand entrepôt voisin. Il souhaitait offrir la demeure à son épouse pour avoir supporté avec lui le dur labeur leur ayant permis de faire prospérer leurs affaires. L'architecte a été fidèle aux requêtes spécifiques de l'épouse du commanditaire visant à la création d'une maison sans barrière, adaptée à leur future vie de couple retraité. La structure devait aussi accommoder confortablement les divers chiens et chats vivant avec la famille. Kawaguchi a utilisé le charbon végétal comme matière première pour gagner du terrain sur la rizière mais aussi contre l'humidité.

Construida en las afueras de la ciudad de Niigata, al lado de un arrozal, esta casa fue diseñada para el propietario de un gran comercio de la zona. Éste quiso construirla para su esposa como regalo o recompensa por los años de duro trabajo que ambos tuvieron que soportar para que su próspero negocio sea lo que es hoy en día. La arquitecta dio salida adecuada a la petición expresa de la propietaria de conseguir una vivienda libre de obstáculos, sobre todo pensada para atender sus futuras necesidades de pareja de avanzada edad. La estructura de la casa también tenía que ser adecuada para albergar a los perros y gatos que conviven con la familia. Kawaguchi usó carbón vegetal como materia básica para construir en terreno ganado al arrozal, así como para reducir los efectos de la humedad.

Architects: **Takaharu + Yui Tezuka / Masahiro Ikeda**

Location: **Tokyo – Japan**

House to Catch the Sky 2

Photographer: **Katsuhisa Kida** Completion date: **2002**

This structure constitutes a simple and original response to its location in a densely populated residential area of Tokyo. One of its most striking features is the positioning of its windows, which have been placed at the eye level of its residents when they are in a sitting position, in order to protect their privacy. So, while the height of the windowpanes is restricted to 2 feet, they are as broad as the structure of the building permits. The skylight in the roof allows sunlight to pour in and adds a sense of contact with the outside world, while still respecting the owners' desire for privacy.

Dieses Gebäude stellt eine originelle und einfache Antwort auf die Herausforderung des Bauens in einem dichtbesiedelten Wohnviertel von Tokio dar. Das Hauptmerkmal liegt in der Positionierung der Fenster, mit der die Privatsphäre der Bewohner garantiert werden soll: Sie liegen exakt in Augenhöhe, wenn die Personen sitzen. Während die Fensterscheiben in ihrer Höhe auf 60 cm begrenzt sind, erstrecken sie sich in ihrer Breite so weit wie die Struktur des Gebäudes es zulässt. Reichlich Sonnenlicht dringt durch das Dachfenster, welches vor fremden Blicken schützt und doch eine gewisse Verbindung mit der Außenwelt herstellt.

Cette construction est la réponse simple et ultime à un site d'une zone résidentielle densément peuplée de Tokyo. L'élément clé de l'intimité de ses résidents est la hauteur des fenêtres. Elles se trouvent exactement au niveau des yeux des personnes assises. De ce fait, bien que les ouvertures mesurent au plus 60 cm de haut, elles s'élargissent sur toute l'amplitude permise par la construction. La claire-voie du toit diffuse un flot de lumière, préserve l'intimité des habitants et offre une manière d'ouverture sur l'extérieur.

Esta estructura representa una respuesta simple y original al lugar en que se halla ubicada, una zona densamente poblada de Tokio. Una de sus principales características reside en la colocación de sus ventanales. A fin de mantener la intimidad de sus residentes, todas las ventanas han sido emplazadas justo al nivel de la vista de éstos una vez sentados. Así pues, mientras la altura de los cristales es de reducidas dimensiones, 60 cm, su anchura se extiende todo lo que la estructura pueda dar de sí. El tragaluz situado en el tejado facilita el paso de abundante luz solar y proporciona una sensación de apertura al exterior manteniendo el deseo de privacidad de sus propietarios.

Architects: **Takaharu + Yui Tezuka / Masahiro Ikeda**

Location: **Tokyo – Japan**

Anthill House

Photographer: **Katsuhisa Kida** Completion date: **2001**

In response to the small triangular site on which the building is located, the architects decided to position the stairs right on the perimeter of the site in order to maximize its central living space. The result, a spiral staircase winding up through the different floors, is one of the most distinctive elements in this project. The circular layout of the house, which creates a variable four-floor setting, is reminiscent of the path followed by ants burrowing inside a discarded apple. Each floor has been allotted a different color—blue, red, green or yellow—and these heighten the identity and personality of the house's owner, a director of cartoon films.

Um den kleinen dreieckigen Bauplatz dieses Gebäudes optimal auszunutzen und den zentralen Wohnraum zu vergrößern, wurde die Treppe entlang der Außenwand des Hauses platziert. Die so entstandene, sich durch die verschiedenen Stockwerke erstreckende, Wendeltreppe ist der Blickfang dieses Projektes. Die kreisförmige Organisation des Hauses schafft eine in sich variierte vierstöckige Struktur und erinnert an eine Ameisenstraße, die sich durch einen weggeworfenen Apfel arbeitet. Die in jedem Stockwerk unterschiedlichen Farben Blau, Rot, Grün und Gelb verstärken die Identität und Persönlichkeit des Besitzers, ein Regisseur für Zeichentrickfilme.

En réponse au petit espace triangulaire accueillant l'édifice, les architectes ont décidé de placer les escaliers juste au périmètre du site, maximisant ainsi l'espace de vie central. Les escaliers en spirale résultants, s'insinuant dans les étages, peuvent être décrit comme l'un des éléments clés du projet. L'organisation circulaire de la maison, créant un décor variable sur quatre niveaux, rappelle le chemin des fourmis cherchant à dévorer une pomme délaissée. Diverses couleurs par étage – bleu, rouge, vert et jaune – soulignent l'identité et la personnalité du propriétaire, un réalisateur de dessins animés.

Como reacción al emplazamiento de este edificio, ubicado en un reducido solar triangular, los arquitectos optaron por situar la escalera bordeando el perímetro del terreno para así poder potenciar al máximo el espacio vital central. La resultante y sinuosa escalera de caracol serpenteando a lo largo de los diferentes pisos de la casa es uno de los elementos distintivos del proyecto. La organización circular de la casa, que crea un marco o entorno variable de cuatro pisos, recuerda en cierto modo a la trayectoria seguida por las hormigas carcomiendo el interior de una manzana en deshecho. Los colores azul, rojo, verde y amarillo asignados a cada uno de los pisos contribuyen a realzar la identidad y personalidad de su propietario, un director de filmes de dibujos animados.

Architect: **Shoji Terabayashi**

Location: **Tokyo – Japan**

Ya Ya Ya

Photographer: **Shoji Terabayashi** Completion date: **2002**

The last "Ya" character in "Ya Ya Ya" represents house in Japanese. Ya Ya House is situated in the western suburbs of Greater Tokyo, and it is owned by a businessman and his wife, who is a professional musician. The owners fell in love with this area because it still contains many open spaces with fields and gardens. When they commissioned the project, they told the architect that their vision of a perfect house was best reflected by the simplicity of Louis Kahn's Escherick House in Pennsylvania. Shoji Terabayashi then came up with a design which, although respecting the spirit of the couple's model, strayed from the modern idiom to conjure up settings reminiscent of the 1960s.

Das letzte Schriftzeichen „Ya" von „Ya Ya Ya" bedeutet auf japanisch Haus. Das Ya Ya Haus befindet sich in einem der westlichen Vororte von Tokio und wird von einem Ehepaar – ein Geschäftsmann und eine Musikerin – bewohnt. Den Eigentümern gefiel das Grundstück, weil es in seiner Umgebung noch viele Felder und Gärten gibt. Bei der Auftragsvergabe legten die Eigentümer dem Architekten ihre Vorstellung eines idealen Hauses dar, welches sie am besten in der Einfachheit des von dem Architekten Louis Kahn erbauten Escherick-Hauses in Pennsylvania verwirklicht sahen. Auf diesem Konzept beruhend, entwarf Shoji Terabayashi ein Haus, dessen Wohnräume entgegen der modernen Formensprache an die Ästhetik der 1960er Jahre erinnern.

Le dernier caractère « Ya » de « Ya Ya Ya » symbolise la maison en japonais. La maison Ya Ya se situe dans les faubourgs ouest de Tokyo. Ses propriétaires sont un couple d'homme d'affaires et de musicienne. Le couple a aimé le site, en raison des champs et jardins environnants. En commandant le projet à l'architecte, il lui ont transmis leur conception de la maison idéale et préférée, symbolisée par la simplicité de la maison Escherick de Louis Kahn en Pennsylvanie. Shoji Terabayashi a produit, s'appuyant sur cette idée, une maison évoquant la nostalgie des espaces des années 1960.

El último ideograma de la frase "Ya Ya Ya" representa una casa en japonés. Hablando, entonces, de la Casa Ya Ya, ésta se halla ubicada en un suburbio de la parte oeste del Gran Tokio. La habita un matrimonio formado por un empresario y su esposa, músico de profesión. Se enamoraron de esta zona de Tokio porque en ella quedan aún grandes espacios abiertos de campos y jardines. Al encargar el proyecto, transmitieron al arquitecto que su noción de casa ideal quedaba perfectamente reflejada en la simplicidad de la Escherick House, casa del arquitecto Louis Kahn, en Pennsylvania. Shoji Terabayashi presentó entonces un diseño en el que aun manteniendo el espíritu del ideal expuesto se apartaba de lo moderno para evocar espacios reminiscentes de la década de los sesenta.

Architect: **Love the Life**

Location: **Tokyo – Japan**

K-House

Photographer: **Seikoh Fukuma** Completion date: **2002**

Love the Life, a prominent design studio mainly known for its designs of shops, converted this nondescript prefabricated house into an outstanding and cozy living space. As
the initial "K" stands for Kaeru (frog), the architects commissioned a Balinese artist to
design stone statues in the form of frogs. The house's original roof garden, complete with a
pond packed with tiny fish and skates, creates a natural atmosphere with relaxing and typ-
ically Asian touches.

Love the Life, ein berühmtes und hauptsächlich im Bereich der Ladengestaltung tätiges
Designerstudio, hat hier ein gewöhnliches Fertighaus in einen originellen und gemüt-
lichen Lebensraum verwandelt. Da „K" für Kaeru (Frosch) steht, beauftragten die Architekten
einen indonesischen Künstler aus Bali mit dem Entwurf von Froschfiguren aus Stein. Dank
der einzigartigen Dachterrasse mit seinem angelegten und von Rochen und kleineren
Fischen reich bevölkerten Teich wurde eine angenehme und natürliche asiatische
Atmosphäre geschaffen.

Love the Life, un cabinet de design reconnu, principalement pour la création de boutique, a réformé cette maison médiocre et préfabriquée en un lieu de vie original et plaisant. L'initiale « K » signifiant Kaeru (grenouille), les architectes ont chargé un artiste balinais de concevoir des statues de l'animal en pierre. Grâce à un exceptionnel toit paysager où petits poissons et raies d'étang abondent, le lieu offre une sorte d'atmosphère asiatique naturelle tranquille.

Love the Life, un famoso estudio de diseño fundamentalmente activo en el campo del diseño de boutiques, ha sido el encargado de realizar las reformas de esta casa prefabricada, normal y corriente, hasta transformarla en un espacio habitable modélico y agradable. Como la letra K es la inicial del término "kaeru" (rana), los arquitectos encargaron a un artista indonesio de Bali el diseño de esculturas de ranas talladas en piedra. Gracias a su original azotea ajardinada con estanque incluido en el que abundan todo tipo de peces minúsculos y rayas, el escenario adquiere un ambiente asiático relajado y natural.

Architect: **Makoto Koizumi**

Location: **Tokyo – Japan**

Yoshida House

Photographer: **Nacása & Partners Inc.** Completion date: **2000**

Makoto Koizumi is one of Tokyo's leading interior and product designers. His designs range from residential houses to shops, such as the one he drew up for Issey Miyake. In this case, he renovated an unremarkable 4-bedroom, 1,020 sq. ft. apartment for a professional couple—a businessman who works for an auction house and a jewellery designer. In their opinion, entrusting the conversion to Koizumi proved a gratifying experience, as the result was a simple and functional modern space, designed to the tiniest detail with the utmost care. The house seems to resemble a picture frame, within which the owners paint the picture of their own life.

Makoto Koizumi ist einer der führenden Innenarchitekten und Industriedesigner von Tokio, der sowohl Wohnhäuser als auch Geschäfte, wie das für Issey Miyake ausgestaltet. Diese 95 m² große, herkömmliche 4-Zimmer-Wohnung wurde für ein Ehepaar – der Mann arbeitet in einer Auktionsfirma und die Frau ist Goldschmiedin – modernisiert. Für die Eigentümer war es eine positive Erfahrung, sich Koizumis Ästethik anzuvertrauen, da das Ergebnis funktional einfache und moderne Räume sind, in denen alles bis zum kleinsten Detail perfekt ausgestaltet ist. Die Wohnung ähnelt einem Bilderrahmen, in den die Eigentümer ihr eigenes Leben hineinmalen.

Makoto Koizumi est l'un des principaux créateurs d'intérieurs et de produits de Tokyo. Ses concepts vont de résidences en magasins, ainsi celui d'Issey Miyake. Cet appartement de 95 m² pour 4 chambres a été rénové pour un couple, un homme d'affaires d'une société d'enchères et une créatrice de bijoux. Confier la rénovation à Koizumi fut une expérience gratifiante selon les propriétaires, satisfaits de vivre dans un espace moderne, simple et fonctionnel, conçu jusqu'au dernier détail avec une touche de perfection. Cette demeure ressemble à un cadre, les occupants y peignant l'image de leur vie.

Makoto Koizumi es un destacado interiorista y diseñador industrial de Tokio. Su actividad profesional abarca desde casas residenciales hasta tiendas, como la diseñada para Issey Miyake. Este apartamento común y corriente que consta de cuatro habitaciones y 95 m² ha sido renovado y acondicionado para una pareja de profesionales compuesta por una diseñadora de joyería y un empleado de una empresa de subastas. Según los propietarios, ha sido una grata experiencia el haber encomendado las tareas de rehabilitación de su vivienda a Koizumi. El resultado es poder disfrutar de un espacio moderno, simple y funcional, con acabados de calidad llevados hasta el más mínimo detalle. Los dueños de esta vivienda, que podría asemejarse al marco de un cuadro, pintan su propia vida.

Architect: **Makoto Koizumi**

Location: **Tokyo – Japan**

Sumire Aoi House

Photographers: **Murazumi, Souichi** Completion date: **1999**

This small house located in Tokyo is an adaptation of the house the famous architect Makoto Mazuzawa (1925–1990) built for himself in 1952, shortly after World War II, when building materials were still scarce. Sumire and Aoi are the names of its owner's daughters. The main features of this square, two-story house ares the maxim exploitation of the limited space and the emphasis on unifying the interior and exterior spaces. 50 years after Makoto's house was designed, the Japanese are confronting the bursting of their economic bubble and are increasingly adopting a modern lifestyle with a few, carefully selected belongings.

Dieses kleine Haus in Tokio ist eine Überarbeitung des Eigenheims des berühmten Architekten Makoto Mazuzawa (1925–1990), welches 1952, kurz nach dem Krieg errichtet wurde, als Baumaterial knapp war. Sumire und Aoi sind die Töchter des Hausbesitzers. Das Hauptmerkmal dieses zweistöckigen, quadratischen Hauses ist die Maximalisierung des begrenzten Raumes, sowie das Bestreben, den inneren und äußeren Raum zu vereinigen. 50 Jahre nach dem Originalentwurf und in einer wirtschaftlich unbeständigen Periode wissen die Japaner das moderne Leben mit nur wenigen aber sorgsam ausgewählten Attributen zunehmend zu schätzen.

Cette petite maison tokyoïte est une version repensée de la propre demeure du célèbre architecte Makoto Mazuzawa (1925–1990), de 1952, peu après la guerre, alors que les restrictions des matériaux de construction sévissaient encore. Sumire et Aoi sont les noms de filles du propriétaire. La maximisation d'un espace limité et la poursuite de son unification intérieure/extérieure sont les éléments essentiels de cette maison carrée de deux étages. 50 ans après sa conception et l'ère de l'euphorie économique étant révolue, les japonais apprécient mieux un foyer moderne aux effets moins nombreux mais choisis.

Esta pequeña casa ubicada en Tokio representa una versión adaptada de la casa del famoso arquitecto Makoto Mazuzawa (1925–1990), construida en 1952, poco después de la guerra, una época en la que los materiales de construcción escaseaban. Sumire y Aoi son los nombres de las hijas del propietario de esta vivienda. Su principal característica, con sus dos pisos y su diseño cuadrado, es potenciar y aprovechar al máximo sus reducidas dimensiones, buscando asimismo unificar su espacio interior con el exterior. Cincuenta años después de su diseño original, los japoneses se enfrentan al estallido de su burbuja económica, y aprecian cada vez más llevar una vida moderna con pocas pertenencias pero bien seleccionadas.

Architect: **speed studio**

Location: **Kanagawa – Japan**

House in Chigasaki

Photographer: **Kozo Takayama**   Completion date: **2002**

This house near Tokyo and the Pacific Ocean was designed by the young team of architects that form speed studio as both a home and a surfing store for its young owner. The seven rooms that make up this building include a workshop for surfing equipment in the lower basement, while the shop itself takes up the upper basement. On the ground floor there is a bedroom, with the kitchen and tearoom situated on the mezzanine. Finally there is a living room on the first floor and a loft. All the rooms resemble white boxes, both inside and outside, and they are connected to each other by 2-inch wood-framed windows set in the walls. These interconnections unify the design to such an extent that the interior feels almost like a single large room.

Dieses in der Nähe Tokios und des Pazifik gelegene Haus wurde vom jungen Architektenteam speed studio entworfen und dient dem jungen Eigentümer gleichermaßen als Wohnhaus und Surfshop. Zu den sieben Räumen, die sich über das Gebäude verteilen, gehört im untersten Kellergeschoss eine Werkstatt für Surfausstattung und ein Verkaufsraum in der Etage darüber. Im Erdgeschoss befindet sich ein Schlafzimmer, im Zwischengeschoss eine Küche mit Teeraum; der Wohnraum liegt im ersten Stock und schließlich gibt es noch ein Loft. Alle Räume ähneln von außen wie innen weißen Schachteln und sind durch Fenster mit 5 cm dicken Holzrahmen miteinander verbunden. Diese Verknüpfungen vereinheitlichen den Entwurf, so als handle es sich um einen einzigen großen Raum.

Proche de Tokyo et du Pacifique, cette maison, conçue par la jeune équipe d'architectes de speed studio, sert de foyer mais aussi de boutique de surf pour son jeune proprié-taire. Parmi les sept pièces le formant, l'édifice compte un atelier pour l'équipement de surf au sous-sol et la boutique en demi sous-sol. Le rez-de-chaussée accueille une chambre, la cuisine et la salle de thé se trouvant en mezzanine. Enfin le séjour s'invite au premier étage avec un loft. Chaque pièce, semblable à une boîte blanche et ouverte sur l'extérieur et l'in-térieur, est connectée avec ses voisines par des fenêtres au cadre de bois de 5 cm au mur. Cette ouverture interconnectée projette un design d'intérieur unifié formant presque une grande pièce unique.

Esta casa diseñada por el joven equipo de arquitectos speed studio, situada cerca de Tokio y del océano Pacífico, es utilizada por su joven propietario como un espacio con dependencias destinadas a vivienda y a su tienda de surf. De entre las siete habitaciones en que se distribuye la casa, hay un taller para material de surf en el sótano, mientras que la tienda está en el semisótano. En la planta baja encontramos una habitación y la cocina, y en el entresuelo, un salón de té. Finalmente se accede al salón situado en el primer piso, y por último a un loft. Todas las estancias se asemejan a una caja blanca y están conecta-das entre sí mediante ventanas con carpintería de madera de 5 cm, que proyec-tan un inte-riorismo unificado: se tiene la sensación de estar en una sala única grande.

Architect: **Makiko Tsukada**

Location: **Tokyo – Japan**

U&U House

Photographer: **Mitsumasa Fujitsuka (HELICO)**   Completion date: **2000**

Makiko Tsukada, who was born in Hokkaido, has worked for renown architectural studios, such as those of Minoru Takeyama and Shigeru Ban. She established her own studio in 1995. The uniqueness of U&U House is to be found in its structural system, composed of eight large bookshelves made of wood and laminated plywood and designed to hold the huge amount of books owned by its proprietors, a married couple in their thirties with one child. The flow of the space from room to room is achieved by means of these bookshelves, which act as partitions. As the house is situated in a cul-de-sac, the architect built a terrace next to the street in order to obtain greater visual depth.

Die aus Hokkaido stammende Architektin Makiko Tsukada hatte in bekannten Architekturbüros wie Minoru Takeyama und Shigeru Ban gearbeitet, bevor sie 1995 ihr eigenes Büro gründete. Die Einzigartigkeit von U&U House liegt in seiner strukturellen Ordnung: acht große, aus Holz und Sperrholzpaneelen gezimmerte Bücherregale, die den enormen Bücherbestand der Eigentümer, ein Ehepaar in den Dreißigern und ihr Kind, aufnehmen sollen. Das Ineinander-Übergehen der Räume wird durch die verschiedenen Regale, die gleichzeitig als Trennwände dienen, gewährleistet. Da sich das Grundstück in einer Sackgasse befindet, ließ die Architektin gleich neben der Straße eine Terrasse anlegen, um eine größere optische Tiefe zu erzielen.

Makiko Tsukada, native d'Hokkaido, a travaillé pour des cabinets d'architecture de renom ainsi Minoru Takeyama et Shigeru Ban. Elle a lancé son étude en 1995. Le caractère unique de U&U House tient à son système structurel comptant huit grandes étagères en érable contreplaqué et en bois d'œuvre conçues pour accueillir adéquatement l'immense collection de livres des propriétaires, un couple de trentenaires avec un enfant. Le flux de l'espace est assuré entre les pièces par ces étagères servant de cloisons. Le site de la demeure étant un cul-de-sac, l'architecte a pensé une terrasse sur rue afin d'offrir un surcroît de profondeur visuelle.

Makiko Tsukada, natural de Hokkaido, ha trabajado para conocidos talleres de arquitectura como los de Minoru Takeyama y Shigeru Ban. Posteriormente, en 1995, fundó su propio estudio. La singularidad de la casa U&U estriba en su sistema estructural, compuesto por ocho grandes estanterías de madera y lámina de contrachapado diseñadas para colocar la inmensa cantidad de libros que posee su familia propietaria, formada por un matrimonio treintañero con un hijo. La fluidez del espacio entre las diversas estancias se consigue mediante dichas estanterías, que hacen la función de tabiques. Al estar el solar de la casa ubicado en una calle sin salida, el arquitecto proyectó una terraza al lado de la calle con el fin de obtener una mayor profundidad visual.

Architect: **Hideyuki Yamashita, Infagenda Ltd.**

Location: **Ishioka – Japan**

TM-House

Photographer: **Hideyuki Yamashita** Completion date: **January 2002**

Hideyuki Yamashita, the boss of Infagenda Inc., studied under Kazuo Shinohara and Peter Cook. He then worked for Nikken Sekkei and the Richard Rogers Partnership in London and Tokyo. In TM-House, full-width sliding doors are installed in the south elevation of a two-story reinforced concrete structure. Both architect and client opted for concrete not only for structural purposes but also in order to achieve the transparency that would provide expansive views from the southwestern facade. The W-structure connecting the ground and the roof acts as a truss, allowing both sides to open freely. Inside, the concrete surfaces create a cool and solid perception of space.

Hideyuki Yamashita, Direktor von Infagenda Inc., studierte bei Kazuo Shinohara und Peter Cook. Später arbeitete er bei Nikken Sekkei und für Richard Rogers Partnership in London und Tokio. In TM-House wurden Schiebetüren in die gesamte nach Süden gerichtete Fassade dieses zweistöckigen Gebäudes aus Stahlbeton eingelassen. Architekt und Bauherr haben sich nicht nur aus bautechnischen Gründen für Stahlbeton entschieden, sondern auch wegen der dadurch erzielten Transparenz, die einen weiten Ausblick von der Südwestseite aus ermöglicht. Die wie ein Gerüst wirkende W-förmige Struktur verbindet Boden und Decke, sodass beide Seiten frei und offen bleiben konnten. Im Hausinnern vermitteln die Oberflächen aus Beton ein kühles und massives Raumgefühl.

Hideyuki Yamashita, le patron de Infagenda Inc., a étudié auprès de Kazuo Shinohara et Peter Cook. Puis il a travaillé chez Nikken Sekkei et avec Richard Rogers Partnership à Londres et Tokyo. Pour TM-House, des portes coulissantes de pleine largeur sont installées dans l'élévation sud d'une structure en béton armé de deux niveaux. Architecte et client ont choisi le béton pour des motifs structurels mais aussi pour créer la transparence générant de vastes vues sur la façade sud-ouest. La structure en W liant sol et poutres joue les armatures permettant la libre ouverture de chaque côté. À l'intérieur, toutes les surfaces en béton créent une perception froide et solide de l'espace.

Hideyuki Yamashita, director de Infagenda Inc., estudió bajo la tutela de Kazuo Shinohara y de Peter Cook. Posteriormente trabajó para Nikken Sekkei y para Richard Rogers Partnership en sus oficinas de Tokio y Londres. En TM-House, el arquitecto instaló puertas correderas de apertura total en la fachada de la parte sur de esta estructura de hormigón. Dicho material fue el que tanto el arquitecto como su cliente eligieron no sólo por cuestiones estructurales sino también para lograr la transparencia que permitiera disfrutar de una amplia panorámica desde su fachada sudoeste. La estructura en forma de W que une el suelo con el tejado apuntala un entramado en donde ambas partes se abren libremente. En su interior toda la superficie de hormigón provoca una sensación de espacio frío y sólido.

Architect: **Atelier Bow Wow**

Location: **Tokyo – Japan**

Mini House

Photographer: **Shigeru Hiraga** Completion date: **1999**

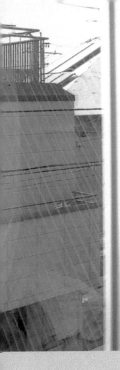

Momoyo Kaijima and Yoshiharu Tsukamoto established Atelier Bow Wow in 1992 and they are now both teaching in Japanese universities. They are well-known not only as architects but also for their famous research project called "Made in Tokyo". This project is an exhaustively documented collection, complete with photos and axonometric projections, of a host of buildings designed in a kitsch style of dubious taste that is also fascinatingly strange and amusing, and highly typical of Japan. A "Horse" apartment, a "Pachinko" cathedral, "Karaoke" hotels, a "Graveyard" road (a tunnel running under a cemetery) are just a few of the countless weird constructions featured in "Made in Tokyo". Atelier Bow Wow's housing projects always seek to respond—as in the case of this Mini House—to the circumstances of their location and surroundings.

Momoyo Kaijima und Yoshiharu Tsukamoto gründeten das Atelier Bow Wow 1992 und lehren jetzt an japanischen Universitäten. Bekannt sind sie nicht nur als Architekten, sondern auch wegen ihres Forschungsprojektes „Made in Tokyo". Dieses Projekt beinhaltet eine Fülle von Daten, Fotos und axonometrische Projektionen von dubiosen aber gleichzeitig auch faszinierend fremdartigen, witzigen und kitschigen Gebäuden und Räumen, die wahrscheinlich nur in Japan zu finden sind. Ein „Pferd"-Apartment, eine „Pachinko"-Kathedrale, „Karaoke"-Hotels, eine „Friedhof"-Straße, – ein unter einem Friedhof verlaufender Tunnel –, sind nur einige der endlosen, sonderbaren Projekte, die hier unter dem Siegel „Made in Tokyo"" zusammengetragen wurden. Die von Atelier Bow Wow konzipierten Wohnprojekte setzen sich immer mit den Vorgaben des Standorts und der Umgebung auseinander und stellen – wie auch hier in Mini House – entsprechende Antworten vor.

Momoyo Kaijima et Yoshiharu Tsukamoto ont créé Atelier Bow Wow en 1992 et ils enseignent désormais à l'université, au Japon. Ils sont aujourd'hui reconnus, non seulement comme des architects mais aussi pour leur célèbre projet de recherche baptisé « Made in Tokyo ». Le projet fourmille de données, photos et projections axonométriques d'immeubles et d'espaces discutables mais aussi étrangement fascinants, amusants et kitsch, existant probablement uniquement au Japon. Un appartement « Cheval », une cathédrale « Pachinko », des hôtels « Karaoke », une route « Cimetière » – tunnel de circulation sous un sanctuaire – sont quelques unes des innombrables constructions bizarres de « Made in Tokyo ». Les projets de logement d'Atelier Bow Wow tendent toujours à répondre, ainsi Mini House, à une situation et à un environnement.

Momoyo Kaijima y Yoshiharu Tsukamoto fundaron el taller de arquitectura Bow Wow en 1992, y actualmente los dos ejercen la docencia en universidades japonesas. Kaijima y Tsukamoto han adquirido renombre, no tan sólo como arquitectos, sino también por su famoso proyecto de investigación conocido con el nombre de "Made in Tokyo". El proyecto es una recopilación, con abundante información, fotografías y proyecciones axonométricas, de un sinnúmero de edificios de dudosa estética kitsch, a la vez divertidos e imbuidos de una fascinante rareza, muy propios de Japón. Un apartamento "Caballo", una catedral "Pachinko", hoteles "Karaoke" o una carretera "Cementerio" –un túnel construido bajo un cementerio– son algunas de las innumerables construcciones que aparecen en "Made in Tokyo". Los proyectos residenciales de Bow Wow siempre buscan dar respuesta, como en Mini House, a una particular situación con referencia a su ubicación y entorno.

Architect: **Shigeru Ban Architects**

Location: **Nishinomiya – Japan**

House 2/5

Photographer: **Hiroyuki Hirai** Completion date: **1995**

Shigeru Ban studied at the Southern California Institute of Architecture and the Cooper Union in New York. After working for Arata Isozaki, the architect set up his own studio in 1985. His most outstanding recent projects include "The Naked House", the Japanese pavilion for EXPO 2000 in Hanover and his contribution to "The Commune by The Great Wall" project in Beijing in 2002. The theme of this housing project can be appreciated by looking at the ground plan of its lower floor. The architect has divided this piece of land measuring 40 x 66 feet into five identical oblong strips, alternating two interior spaces with three exteriors converted into gardens and terraces. Various different settings and spaces can be created by adjusting its mobile elements according to the season, the weather or the time of day.

Shigeru Ban studierte am Southern California Institute of Architecture und an der Cooper Union in New York. Nach Zusammenarbeit mit Arata Isozaki gründete der Architekt 1985 sein eigenes Büro. Zu seinen bekanntesten Projekten in jüngster Zeit zählen „The Naked House", der japanische Pavillion für die EXPO 2000 in Hannover und seine Teilnahme an dem 2002 in Peking ausgeführten Projekt „The Commune by The Great Wall". Ein Blick auf den Grundriss des Erdgeschosses macht die eigentliche Idee dieses Hauses verständlich. Der Architekt teilte das Baugrundstück von 15 m Breite und 25 m Länge in fünf gleichmäßige, rechteckige Abschnitte, von denen abwechselnd zwei als Wohnfläche und drei als Gärten und Terrassen genutzt werden. Dank dem Einsatz von beweglichen Elementen kann man je nach Jahreszeit, Wetter oder Tageszeit die Raumaufteilung und -gestaltung variieren.

Shigeru Ban a étudié au Southern California Institute of Architecture et à la Cooper Union de New York. Sa collaboration avec Arata Isozaki a été suivie de la création de son propre cabinet en 1985. Parmi ses projets récents et connus, il convient de souligner « The Naked House », le pavillon japonais pour l'EXPO 2000 de Hanovre et sa participation à « The Commune by The Great Wall » à Beijing, en 2002. Le thème de ce projet de logement s'apprécie en observant le plan au sol de son rez-de-chaussée. L'architecte divise ce terrain de 15 m de large sur 25 m de long en cinq bandes oblongues similaires, faisant alterner deux espaces intérieurs et trois extérieurs convertis en jardins et terrasses. Divers types de décors et espaces différents sont possibles en utilisant les éléments mobiles selon la saison, le climat, l'heure.

Shigeru Ban estudió Arquitectura en el Southern California Institute of Architecture y en la Cooper Union de Nueva York. Después de trabajar con Arata Isozaki, fundó su propio estudio en 1985. Entre sus proyectos más conocidos de reciente creación destacan "The Naked House", el pabellón japonés para la Expo 2000 de Hannover y su participación, en el 2002 en Pekín, en el proyecto conocido como "The Commune by The Great Wall". La idea principal de este proyecto residencial se puede apreciar en los planos de la planta baja. El arquitecto divide la superficie de este solar de 15 m de ancho por 25 m de profundidad en cinco franjas rectangulares iguales, e intercala dos espacios interiores con tres exteriores convertidos en jardines y terrazas. Mediante elementos movibles según la estación, el clima o la hora del día en que se encuentre, su propietario puede crear diferentes ambientaciones.

Architects: **Hiroyuki Arima + Urban Fourth**

Location: **Fukuoka – Japan**

3R House

Photographer: **Koji Okamoto** Completion date: **1997**

Hiroyuki Arima studied in Kyoto. In the 1990s he founded the architectural studio Urban Fourth, he divides his time between Tokyo and Fukuoka, and his work ranges from interior design to city planning. This apartment is conceived as a continuous space, with no fixed partitions. The name "3R" refers to the three movable panels placed near the entrance to the apartment. By folding them at different angles, the space may be modified to provide a wide range of different combinations, depending on the needs and tastes of each resident. The furniture was removed and the walls, floors and ceilings were painted white to enhance as far as possible the low intensity of the sunlight that enters from the north. The rooms run into each other smoothly on both floors, with a staircase linking the two levels.

Hiroyuki Arima studierte in Kyoto und gründete in den 1990er Jahren das Architekturbüro Urban Fourth. Er ist in Tokio und Fukuoka auf allen Gebieten, von der Innenarchitektur bis zur Stadtplanung, tätig. Dieses Apartment wurde als ein ununterbrochener Raum ohne feste Einteilungen konzipiert. Sein Name „3R" beruht auf den drei verstellbaren Trennwänden nahe der Eingangstür. Je nach Geschmack oder Bedürfnis des Bewohners kann durch Verstellen und Drehen der einzelnen Wände eine Fülle von verschiedenen Raumkombinationen geschaffen werden. Die Möbel wurden beseitigt und der Boden, die Wände und Decken weiß gestrichen, um so den schwachen Lichteinfall von Norden zu optimieren. Die einzelnen Räume gehen auf beiden mit einer Treppe verbundenen Stockwerken sanft ineinander über.

Hiroyuki Arima a étudié à Kyoto. Dans les années 1990, il a fondé le cabinet Urban Fourth. Il alterne son travail entre le design d'intérieur et l'urbanisme, à Tokyo comme à Fukuoka. Cet appartement est conçu en un espace continu, sans partition fixe. Le nom « 3R » se réfère aux trois panneaux mobiles placés près de l'entrée du logement. En les pliant à différents angles, l'espace est modifiable pour offrir une foule de combinaisons, selon les besoins et les goûts de chaque résident. Le mobilier a été retiré et les murs, sols et plafonds peints en blanc pour mettre en valeur autant que possible le peu de lumière s'infiltrant par le nord. Les pièces se succèdent de manière fluide à chaque étage, liés par un escalier.

Hiroyuki Arima estudió en Kyoto y durante la década de los noventa fundó el estudio Urban Fourth. Hoy compagina su trabajo, que incluye interiorismo y urbanismo, entre Tokio y Fukuoka. Este apartamento ha sido concebido como un espacio ininterrumpido, sin tabiques fijos. Su nombre, 3R, hace referencia a los tres paneles movibles próximos a la entrada. Al plegarse bajo diferentes ángulos, el resultado es un espacio que puede ser modificado, lo que permite innumerables combinaciones según las necesidades y gustos de cada residente. Se retiró el mobiliario, y el techo, las paredes y el suelo se pintaron de blanco para realzar al máximo la poca intensidad de luz natural que entra desde el lado norte. Las estancias se suceden una tras otra en los dos pisos, conectados por unas escaleras.

Architect: **Akira Sakamoto Architects & Associates**

Location: **Osaka – Japan**

House Hakuei

Photographer: **Nacása & Partners Inc.**   Completion date: **1996**

House Hakuei, the architect's own residence, has been awarded many prizes. Its structure comprises one slab of wall combined with three rectangular, parallel elements. The motion of the sunlight projected from above on to a white wall in the interior represents nature and the unstoppable passing of time. The striking beauty and modernity of Sakamoto's houses, which are in some ways reminiscent of minimalist art, are designed to make their inhabitants feel not only comfortable but also mentally and spiritually enriched. His architecture evokes peacefulness, stillness and meditation.

House Hakuei, von dem Architekten selbst bewohnt, wurde mit vielen Preisen ausgezeichnet. Seine Struktur besteht aus einer mit drei quaderförmigen Baukörpern verbundenen Wandscheibe. Das Wandern des Tageslichts, welches von außen auf eine weiße Innenwand fällt, spiegelt die Natur und das unaufhaltsame Vergehen der Zeit wieder. Die große Schönheit und Modernität der Häuser von Sakamoto, die in gewisser Weise an minimalistische Kunstwerke erinnern, geben dem Bewohner nicht nur das Gefühl von Komfort, sondern auch von mentalem und spirituellem Reichtum. Seine Architektur vermittelt inneren Frieden, Ruhe und Meditation.

House Hakuei, la résidence de l'architecte, a reçu nombre de prix. Sa structure comprend une couche de mur combinée à trois volumes parallélépipédiques. Le mouvement de la lumière naturelle projetée de l'extérieur sur le mur blanc de son espace intérieur représente la nature et le passage irrémédiable du temps. La beauté et la modernité intenses des maisons de Sakamoto, similaires à des œuvres minimalistes, offrent aux résidents une sensation de confort mais aussi de richesse mentale et spirituelle. Son architecture engendre la paix de l'esprit, le calme et la méditation.

El proyecto de House Hakuei, la vivienda del propio arquitecto, ha sido galardonado con muchos premios. Su estructura está formada por una lámina de pared combinada con tres paralelepípedos rectangulares. El movimiento de luz natural proyectada desde el exterior hacia una pared blanca situada dentro de la casa representa la naturaleza y el paso imparable del tiempo. Una intensa belleza y su modernidad hacen que las casas de Sakamoto, que en cierta manera recuerdan obras minimalistas, sean concebidas como espacios en los que sus habitantes no sólo sientan comodidad, sino que también les proporcionen riqueza espiritual y mental. Su arquitectura infunde paz interior e invita a la calma y a la meditación.

Other Designpocket titles by teNeues

African Interior Design 3-8238-4563-2
Airline Design 3-8327-9055-1
Bathroom Design 3-8238-4523-3
Beach Hotels 3-8238-4566-7
Berlin Apartments 3-8238-5596-4
Boat Design 3-8327-9054-3
Café & Restaurant Design 3-8327-9017-9
Car Design 3-8238-4561-6
Cool Hotels 3-8238-5556-5
Cool Hotels Africa/Middle East 3-8327-9051-9
Cool Hotels America 3-8238-4565-9
Cool Hotels Asia/Pacific 3-8238-4581-0
Cool Hotels Europe 3-8238-4582-9
Cosmopolitan Hotels 3-8238-4546-2
Country Hotels 3-8238-5574-3
Food Design 3-8327-9053-5
Furniture Design 3-8238-5575-1
Garden Design 3-8238-4524-1
Italian Interior Design 3-8238-5495-X
Kitchen Design 3-8238-4522-5
London Apartments 3-8238-5558-1
Los Angeles Houses 3-8238-5594-8
Miami Houses 3-8238-4545-4
New Scandinavian Design 3-8327-9052-7
Office Design 3-8238-5578-6
Pool Design 3-8238-4531-4
Product Design 3-8238-5597-2
Rome Houses 3-8238-4564-0
San Francisco Houses 3-8238-4526-8
Ski Hotels 3-8238-4543-8
Spa & Wellness Hotels 3-8238-5595-6
Sport Design 3-8238-4562-4
Staircase Design 3-8238-5572-7
Sydney Houses 3-8238-4525-X
Tropical Houses 3-8238-4544-6

Each volume:
12.5 x 18.5 cm, 5 x 7 in.
400 pages
c. 400 color illustrations